Paul Weller &  n

Copyright © 1999 Omn
(A Division of Book Sale

Edited by Rob Dim
Cover & Book designed by Hilite Design
Picture research by Nikk.

ISBN: 0.7119.6818.7
Order No: OP48057

Exclusive Distributors:
Book Sales Limited, 8/9 Frith Street, London W1V 5TZ, UK.
Music Sales Corporation, 257 Park Avenue South, New York, NY 10010, USA.
Five Mile Press, 22 Summit Road, Noble Park, Victoria 3174, Australia.

To the Music Trade only:
Music Sales Limited, 8/9, Frith Street, London W1V 5TZ, UK.

Photo credits:
Front cover: Andy Earl/Retna; back cover: Harry Goodwin. All other pictures
supplied by LFI, Rex Features & Brian Rasic.

Every effort has been made to trace the copyright holders of the photographs in this book but one or two were
unreachable. We would be grateful if the photographers concerned would contact us.

Printed in Great Britain by Printwise (Haverhill) Limited, Suffolk

A catalogue record for this book is available from the British Library.

Visit Omnibus Press at http://www.omnibuspress.com

OMNIBUS PRESS
LONDON · NEW YORK · SYDNEY

CONTENTS

INTRODUCTION

Paul Weller has epitomised different aspects of pop culture over the years. To anyone with an eye for the Mod cloth, he has been a fashion icon. To those involved in left-wing politics in the 1980s, he was one of the few pop stars brave enough to rally to their cause. To thirty-something Jam fans, he fronted the most exciting and vital band since the 1960s (or ever, for that matter). And in the 1990s, he has come to symbolise a very British style of rock which transcends age and easy classification.

But he is also, first and foremost, a very talented songwriter. He is responsible for a canon of work unmatched among his (punk) generation, and performs with an unbridled conviction and energy unsurpassed for a man who reached his fortieth birthday in mid-1998.

To quote the available statistics which support Weller's enormous and prolonged success would be irrelevant here. Instead, this book concentrates on the recorded legacy of Paul Weller's songbook, a soundtrack to a thousand council houses and playgrounds, coffee bars and clubs, public houses and concerts. Put the needle on the record…

THE JAM: STUDIO ALBUMS

IN THE CITY

DATE: MAY 1977

CHART POSITION: NO. 20

ORIGINAL LP: POLYDOR 2383 447

CURRENT CD: POLYDOR 537 417-2

Had Paul Weller not seen the Sex Pistols in summer 1976, it's unlikely The Jam would ever have escaped their suburban Surrey backwater of Woking. As it was, punk fired the headstrong teenager into action. Although still small, the movement seemed inextricably linked with his growing fascination with London itself – and tallied with his love of that older but equally urban cult, Mod.

Thereafter, The Jam (Weller, alongside bassist Bruce Foxton and drummer Rick Buckler) swiftly established themselves within the front rank of punk bands – but they were never punk, nor were they accepted as such by the punk cognoscenti. Instead, they seemed to fit more comfortably under the soon-to-be-coined 'new wave' banner. The Jam signed to Polydor on 15th February 1977 and were rushed into the company's Stratford Place Studios to record their début album with producer Chris Parry (who was instrumental in signing them) and engineer Vic Smith.

On 29th April, The Jam's first single, 'In The City', reached the shops and made the Top 40 – matching the success of peers like the Sex Pistols, The Stranglers and The Clash. *In The City* – the album – arrived the following month. It was very much a product of its time:

Weller's 'Fire And Skill' motto just about summed up its feel.

Jamie Reid's cut-and-paste 'punk' designs for the Pistols inspired Bill Smith's cover: a stark, urban, monochrome image of the band and a back cover showing Sellotape strips and broken tiles, with the distinctive Jam logo sprayed with an aerosol can, graffiti-like against a white tiled backdrop. *In The City* effectively captured the intensity, passion and aggression of their live shows, its twelve songs clocking in at barely over half-an-hour. Weller, who was just approaching his nineteenth birthday, seemed to epitomise the angry young man. His manner was serious and angry, his voice sometimes strained and never relaxed, attracting such adjectives from critics as "hurried", "bleak", "chaotic", "intense" and "highly charged".

But The Jam's real potential lay in Weller's musical background. He had formed The Jam at school with a copy of *The Beatles' Songbook* under one arm and a list of fixtures at the local working men's club under the other. So

Weller's songwriting was rooted in strong melodies and The Jam had evolved into a tight unit on stage. And this is crystal clear on the album, despite its frenetic energy and unpolished production.

The album's main debt (aside from punks pioneers The Clash and the Sex Pistols) was early Who, not least with a cover of the 'Batman Theme'. Paul had discovered The Who's first album (*My Generation*, from 1965) back in late 1974, after hearing the title track on the soundtrack to *Stardust*. His songwriting and guitar playing – and The Jam's whole Mod image of black three-button suits, skinny ties and pointed two-tone spats – stemmed from that LP. (Weller later joked that every song on *In The City* could be linked to an equivalent on *My Generation*). Their live set also included Who songs like 'So Sad About Us' (later a Jam B-side), 'Heatwave' (another track The Jam later recorded, a Motown classic favoured by The Who), and 'Much Too Much'.

Weller's other obsession was Sixties

soul, which prompted the inclusion on the album of Larry Williams' 'Slow Down' (via The Beatles), while their gigs featured such classics as Arthur Conley's 'Sweet Soul Music', The Supremes' 'Back In My Arms Again' and Wilson Pickett's 'In The Midnight Hour' (again, a later album track) and 'Mustang Sally'. And the final influence dated from early 1975, when Paul's guitar technique was inspired by hearing Dr. Feelgood's clenched R&B – and in particular, their guitarist Wilko Johnson's style of combining rhythm and lead.

ART SCHOOL

'Art School' was punchy three-chord punk – brutal, brusque and bludgeoning but still rooted in Sixties beat. Weller was probably inspired by reading about the educational establishments attended by heroes like Pete Townshend, Ray Davies and John Lennon, and updated the idea of the art school as a hotbed of youthful, creative freedom and rebellious expression. In other words, the new art school was punk/new wave.

In 'Art School', the line, "Time is motion and the hands are fast", is not only punning but both fits the pace of the music and vividly illustrates the feelings of excitement and youthful change Weller's trying to portray. He's aware of his own difficulties with self-expression: "Young words are mumbled/They don't always last". The song's themes of rebellion ("Don't need permission for everything that you want") and insecurity ("Never worry if people laugh at you") are commonplace in early Jam songs.

I'VE CHANGED MY ADDRESS

If it was possible to match *In The City* to *My Generation*, then 'I've Changed My Address' echoed the message of The Who's 'Much Too Much' – of giving a girlfriend the shove when marriage beckons. Again, Weller expressed youthful freedom, unshackled by the responsibilities of adulthood, a universal

theme since the dawn of rock'n'roll. The song is one of the album's more melodic tunes, but takes a more threatening turn halfway through, breaking into feed-backing power chords for an angry retort: "No-one's gonna tie me down/Nobody tells me what to do."

SLOW DOWN

The first of two Sixties covers on the album was Larry Williams' U.S. R&B classic, 'Slow Down', issued in Britain as the B-side to 'Dizzy Miss Lizzy' in 1958. Both songs were covered in 1964 by The Beatles – indeed, Paul no doubt discovered the song via their *Long Tall Sally* EP.

The Jam's version might have veered towards pedestrian pub rock had it not been tackled at such a ferocious pace. Idealistic critics slammed The Jam for paying such respectful lip service to the past. Weller responded by wearing a plaque around his neck onstage which read: "How can I be a fucking revivalist when I'm only 18".

I GOT BY IN TIME

Tamla Motown had a strong influence on The Jam but didn't always translate well into their music. An exception was 'I Got By In Time', although it struggled to rise above a messy, 'live' production. Its Vandellas-like, 'Charleston' Motown rhythm, a strong melody and telling lyrics make this one of the forgotten gems of the early Jam repertoire.

At first, it sounds like a straightforward, nostalgic tale of an old flame, but there's more to it. "Some guy that I used to know/Man, he changed so much", sang Weller, "He was my best friend a few years ago, truly inseparable, we were young and full of ideas/But something happened, I don't know why..." It's fair to assume the friend in question was Steve Brookes, who'd formed The Jam with Paul half a decade earlier. 'I Got By In Time' was written around 1975, probably a few months after Brookes left the band – and his friendship with Paul – behind.

Incidentally, The Nips, fronted by Jam fan No. 1, Shane MacGowan, later reworked 'I Got By In Time' into 'Infatuation'.

AWAY FROM THE NUMBERS

'Away From The Numbers' was the album's apex, its one true masterpiece. From the gut-wrenching opening power chords, all the tension, power, urgency and melodic skill that came to be Jam trademarks were focused within this compelling, claustrophobic track. Along with 'Sounds From The Street', its relatively slow pace helped counteract some of the album's unnecessary punk bluster. Both tunes, in fact, were among Paul's newest, with the shared inspiration of surf music: the mid-Sixties Who had indulged in the odd Jan & Dean cover. London had offered an alternative to predictable, suburban Woking life, 'Away From The Numbers' was Weller's pledge to escape from that same home counties drudgery: "Sick and tired of my little niche/I'm gonna break away and find what life is".

Beach Boys-influenced backing harmonies drifted over a subtle,

dreamy middle eight, before the song ended with a descending four-note riff which Weller returned to on several occasions, with the band chanting "Reality so hard" in mantra-like fashion. Genius. 'Numbers' was derisory Sixties Mod slang for the horde of younger mods, so-named because of the vogue for T-shirts sporting big printed digits. This term had spawned The Who's original monicker, the High Numbers – Weller had obviously done his homework.

BATMAN THEME

The theme to the ultimate Sixties TV series was composed by Neal Hefti, but Weller had heard it beefed up by The Who on their 1966 EP, *Ready Steady Who*. *Batman* was immensely popular that year and its cartoon quality perfectly suited The Who's dabblings with pop-art. Pop-art designs have continually graced Weller's record sleeves ever since – and there's also the experimental 'Pop-Art Poem' from 1980. The 'Batman Theme' was a popular encore for The Jam in '77, but their performance – unlike The Who's – was a straightforward garage punk romp that hasn't dated well.

IN THE CITY

Weller wrote 'In The City There's A Thousand Things I Wanna Say To You' (as it was originally entitled) as a tribute to the excitement of Punk London. The song began with an angry, stabbing three-chord guitar riff, before Foxton's pounding, descending bass-line kicked in and Buckler's snare-drum roll signalled the start of the song proper. It mirrored the live Jam sound – harsh and energetic, but still rooted in melody.

A middle eight began with the sound of plectrum scraping against strings to create an atonal burst reminiscent of the second half of The Who's 'Anyway Anyhow Anywhere'. The lyrics owed more to 'My Generation', though proclamations like "I wanna tell you about the young idea", and "But you'd better listen man/Because the kids know where it's at", were clumsier than Townshend's. And the comparisons

didn't stop there: the title (and part of the melody) were borrowed from a 1966 Who song (the B-side to 'I'm A Boy'), a surf-styled number written by drummer Keith Moon and bassist John Entwistle.

Weller was keen to emphasise the line about "a thousand men in uniforms", commenting that the song was "about an innocent victim of police brutality; about the police beating up and killing for no reason." It wasn't – or, at least, that wasn't the main thrust of the lyric – but this is a poignant example of Weller's desire to take the political initiative offered by The Clash's Joe Strummer. Voted 'single-of-the-week' in *NME*, 'In The City' was the fourth British punk/new wave hit. Sex Pistols guitarist Steve Jones later borrowed the main riff for 'Holidays In The Sun'.

SOUNDS FROM THE STREET

'Sounds From The Street' was one of the album's highlights. This celebration of British youth – like 'In The City' – centred on London's nascent punk scene of "young bands playing, young kids diggin'". When Weller sang that famous line, "I know I come from Woking, and you say I'm a fraud/But my heart is in the city, where it belongs," it was difficult not to believe him.

By reaffirming the message of 'In The City', he painted a romantic image of urban life common among (sub)urban kids who look to the country's biggest cities with a kind of awe. His potshot at the Americans, "The U.S.A.'s got the sea/Yeah, but the British kid's got the streets", may have played on the song's West Coast surf influence. Alternatively, Paul may just have been influenced by The Clash's 'I'm So Bored With The U.S.A'.

NON-STOP DANCING

Back in the mid-Seventies, Weller used to attend Northern Soul all-nighters outside Woking. And those visits inspired 'Non-Stop Dancing', after nights spent on uppers, "Truly out of my head/But I ain't sleepy, baby, baby". The song's tuneful mid-Sixties Motown feel was the

most obvious reflection of Weller's Mod obsessions – that line about "the kids are screaming for that James Brown style", and a clumsy attempt at soul/funk guitar.

One particular line, "I don't mind guys trying to compete/I know our love's as strong as the beat", echoed the sentiment of The Who's 'The Kids Are Alright': "I don't mind other guys dancing with my girl". But the song's true substance lay in the final line: "It gives you the feeling that you belong." Like many suburban kids, Weller felt rootless. London gave him a base but Mod gave him a sense of identity, which he has pursued in his music, dress sense, attitude and record buying habits ever since.

TIME FOR TRUTH

'Time For Truth' launched a direct attack on the Labour government of the day, its jibes at "Uncle Jimmy" prompted by Prime Minister James Callaghan's visit to Woking in December 1976. The song also latched onto the death in police custody of suspect Liddle Towers in late

1976, after the coroner's verdict of 'misadventure' led the news media to demand a full enquiry. Towers became a cause célèbre (punk band the Angelic Upstarts wrote their first single about him), although Weller's calls to "bring forward them six pigs/We wanna see them swing so high – Liddle Towers!", lacked political finesse. And lines like "Whatever happened to the great empire?/You bastards have turned it into manure" left much to be desired.

TAKIN' MY LOVE

The B-side of 'In The City' was a more aggressive version of the band's earliest-known recording, punked-up with Paul's most blatant debt to that staccato guitar style popularised by Wilko Johnson. Because of its vintage – Paul wrote the song back in 1973, with help from Steve Brookes – the lyrics were understandably naïve: "Well, come on pretty baby, you know what I like now/You're shakin' all over and it's feeling alright now". The Jam spent their formative years belting out rock'n'roll covers to inebriated locals in and around Woking. But the song's Gene Vincent-isms like "Daddy's little cat's gonna rock all day" were thankfully buried in the mix.

BRICKS AND MORTAR

Paul Weller grew up in Stanley Road, a stone's throw from Woking town centre, which endured a series of upheavals during the Sixties and Seventies. The Wellers moved out of Stanley Road in the late Seventies, but Paul was around long enough to see houses in his street demolished to make way for office buildings; indeed, a redirected road system meant that Stanley Road was halved in length.

All of which explains this lament about the faceless aspects of urban development. "Why do we have to hide our past/By pulling down houses and building parks," barked Weller, "while hundreds are homeless." Such a straightforward, naïve message attracted critical flak, but Weller had a common sense outlook on his world; more sophisticated examinations of social problems came later, when he was more sussed about politics. The music is a typically brash four-chord affair with enough power to match the "yellow bulldozers, the donkey jackets and J.C.B.s" of the song.

NON-ALBUM SONGS

ALL AROUND THE WORLD

After talk of a four-track EP came to nothing, the powerful 'All Around The World' was eventually issued as The Jam's second single in June. It shot to No. 13, maintaining The Jam's status at the forefront of new wave on the back of their first national headlining tour. This was pure, unbridled energy from start to finish, arranged to great effect by producer Chris Parry.

Fanfared by a drum roll, this rallying cry for a "youth explosion" crashed in with an aggressive two-chord guitar attack, and Weller's and Foxton's call-and-response vocals. Over two decades later, 'All Around The World' still sounds like one of the most intense, exciting records of the punk era. The lines, "What's the point in saying destroy/We

want a new life for everyone", and "You can't dismiss what's gone before/But there's foundations for us to explore", drove another wedge between The Jam and the anarchic rhetoric of punk. Weller cemented his ideas about unity that were dotted about In The City with this anthem for a generation: "All around the world, I've been looking for new."

CARNABY STREET

Bassist Bruce Foxton's uneventful ode to that faded West London Mod Mecca of the Sixties was his first composition for the band. In the early Sixties, Carnaby Street had been discovered by London's original Mod hardcore, emerging from its backwater behind Oxford Circus to represent the epitome of Swinging London, with outlandish boutiques full of colourful, ever fancier designs. But this increasing commercialism left it shabby and jaded, and by the late Seventies, it was a hollow tourist attraction.

Hence Foxton's lament, which motors along gamely enough. But his lyrics

haven't dated well: "A part of the British tradition gone down the drain" and "The street that was a part of the British Monarchy" suggest, in hindsight, a naïve patriotism. The song attained a strange irony when, fuelled by The Jam's success and a subsequent Mod Revival, Carnaby Street acted like a hive to a swarm of latter-day Mods, who gravitated to shops selling clothing endorsed by the band.

THE JAM / THIS IS THE MODERN WORLD

THE MODERN WORLD

DATE: NOVEMBER 1977

CHART POSITION: NO. 22

ORIGINAL LP: POLYDOR 2383 475

CURRENT CD: POLYDOR 537 418-2

The Jam's second album has commonly been dismissed as their weakest, and work on the LP was riddled by problems. Initial sessions at an Aylesbury rehearsal studio were abandoned after a week. Then the band relocated to Island's Basing Street Studios in Notting Hill, West London, in September 1977, with a £20,000 advance from Polydor. But the deadline was tight because they were due to fly to America within a few weeks. So the album was rushed – and it showed.

The Modern World was greeted with a barrage of critical animosity. It suffered from lukewarm sales, too, dropping out of the charts more quickly than its predecessor, *In The City*. So too did the lead track, 'This Is The Modern World', which could only scrape to No. 36. Producer Chris Parry (and The Jam themselves) have since agreed with this consensus: in other words, The Jam should have waited, perhaps, until the New Year.

Over two decades on, *The Modern World* deserves a fresh perspective.

For a start, more than any other Jam LP, it caught the band in a state of flux. In half a year, their sound had evolved considerably – and for that alone, the album was an achievement. Weller once spoke of it as their attempt to "cross over" into new wave – "the pop music of the Seventies", as he called it. They were patently keen to progress beyond the punk mould of *In The City*, as evidenced by the Beatle-esque, melodic rush of Paul's slower, more contemplative songs, and a more recognisable Jam 'sound' that revolved around his love of the Rickenbacker guitar.

As to being rushed, well, *In The City* sounds considerably more frantic – but maybe that's no bad thing. This was 1977, after all, a supposed 'year zero' for new bands. No, the real problem with *The Modern World* lay in its inconsistency: some tracks should have been rejected out of hand. But for every cod-new wave blunder (the mindless 'London Traffic' and 'In The Street Today'), the album offered some refreshingly subtle gems.

Paul's old poet friend Dave Waller and Sixties beat poet Adrian Henri were thanked for "foresight and inspiration", directly influencing the lyrics for several songs – as did Ken Kesey's famous tale of life in a sanatorium, *One Flew Over The Cuckoo's Nest*. The album title itself spoke volumes about Weller's views and aspirations. He was both driven to move forward (as in "All around the world I've been looking for new") and still privately fascinated with the 'Mod' in 'Modern'.

On the front cover, the group gazed out from under the Westway (in West London), with bleak-looking council blocks behind them, and Weller wearing a Who badge with Mod-ish arrows stuck on his jumper. The photo was taken by legendary Sixties photographer Gered Mankowitz – the first notable session in which the band weren't dressed uniformly in suits. Together with two songs directly connected with the capital, 'London Traffic' and 'London Girl', this image continued the thread of *In The City* by forging a stark, urban identity for a band blatantly keen to rid themselves of their Surrey roots.

THE MODERN WORLD

On 26th April 1977 – the eve of their début single release – The Jam recorded the first of three BBC radio sessions for John Peel. One of the songs they performed was 'The Modern World', which had once been considered for the B-side to 'All Around The World'. Faintly reminiscent of The Who's 'Pictures Of Lily', the song was inspired by both Weller's Mod obsession and that sense of change that characterised punk.

The lyrics stuck two fingers up to his critics. It began by slating those who thought the writer "knew nothing about the modern world", before climaxing with the final line, "I don't give two fucks about your review" – although the album version was censored on the single to "a damn", an ironic compromise bearing in mind the defiant nature of its message. The final irony was that it stalled at No. 36, although its punchy power chords, nimble bass lines and snappy drumming created a tense atmosphere central to the early Jam sound.

LONDON TRAFFIC

If Bruce Foxton's environmental message pre-empted the pro-public transport lobby by a decade, then it was disgraced by the banality of the music. 'London Traffic' was pedestrian punk (if you pardon the pun) that thrashed along like some two-bit pub rock anthem, though in fairness, the pace disguised some subtle backing harmonies.

STANDARDS

The immediacy of 'Standards' made it a popular live choice. Another sub-Who power chord structure ('I Can't Explain') was matched by an equally basic anti-system/law message and "us and them" theme typical of Weller's early days. The line, "You know what happened to Winston", referred to the main character in Orwell's *1984* rather than Churchill, a pointer to the fact that Weller read more widely than might have been expected.

LIFE FROM A WINDOW

'Mr. B. Cain' – journalist Barry Cain, who later set up *Flexipop* magazine – was thanked for the "teenage blue" phrase in 'Life From A Window'. This was the first evidence of The Jam growing musically, from its more sophisticated structure to its pleasant guitar flourishes.

When he sang, "Up here I can see the world", think of James Cagney's "Look ma! I'm on top of the world", rather than some more literal interpretation (a tower block of the album cover, for example).

Weller was on top of his world: he was a pop star, a position he'd dreamed of for half his life.

THE COMBINE

One of the album's highlights was named after a term used by Ken Kesey in *One Flew Over The Cuckoo's Nest* to describe "the system". The song's angry bite was archetypal early Jam – as was the song's lyrical quest for a sense of identity, dealing with peer pressure and adopting roles in life. Weller expressed a sense of conflict: "I wanna close my eyes and be like the rest" and "I wanna break away but the ties are too strong". In this respect, the song was part of a trilogy, midway between 'Away From The Numbers' (on *In The City*) and 'In The Crowd' (on *All Mod Cons*).

Weller had a knack of cleverly employing day-to-day references: "Sunday papers and the dailys/Ena Sharples, Page 3 girls/News At Ten/War in Rhodesia/Far away in a distant land". Having caught the listener's attention, he then delivers the song's central message: "But we're alright, We're nice and warm here/No one to hurt us – except ourselves."

DON'T TELL THEM YOU'RE SANE

Foxton penned this more blatant interpretation of *One Flew Over The Cuckoo's Nest* to create one of his most compelling songs. Its strength lay in its musical tension, as the band powered through the song, bringing to mind that old cliché, "firing on all cylinders". The figure who's "strapped in his chair, won't go far", is pictured on one of Conny Jude's cartoons on the album's inner sleeve, along with the 'girls' of 'Here Comes The Weekend', the powermongers of 'Standards', a Page 3 girl, a 'London Girl' and other sketches which suggest Weller and his then-girlfriend Gill Price.

IN THE STREET TODAY

Dave Waller received a joint songwriting credit for the otherwise undistinguished 'In The Street Today', for his lines, "Murder on the terraces/Fools in high places/It's all so sickening/And we're so satisfied". These were taken from one of his six untitled poems, which were printed at the back of a Jam songbook in summer '77. "As in all cultures, which hopefully the new wave will evolve into (or maybe it has?), there are a lot of other Art forms," wrote Paul as an introduction, "not only music, but why not new wave painters, playwrights, authors and poets? One such person, and I'm sure there are a lot more, is David Waller, a very talented poet. I relate very deeply to his works. I hope you can." The music was a less inspired, one of the 'problem punk' tracks which captured The Jam at their worst, parodying The Clash, circa 'Career Opportunities'.

LONDON GIRL

Weller was presumably prompted to write this tale of a teenager who'd left home to fend for herself on the streets of London by someone he'd met. The recording sounded rushed but the song had a poignancy that betrayed the writer's tender years (and he was already outstripping his contemporaries). The pace slowed halfway through, the guitar dropping out for a few seconds to make a point.

Weller offered advice in the final verse: "I don't condemn what you've done/I know what it is to be young/You're only searching for today/To seek the answers about yesterday," which might also apply to Weller himself.

I NEED YOU (FOR SOMEONE)

One of the most naked love songs Weller has ever written, 'I Need You (For Someone)' read like a teenage love-letter in places, but then he was only nineteen. The shadow of The Who remained: the song was probably named after a Keith Moon song, from their *A Quick One* album, a link retained in the backing vocals and the melody – especially in the chorus. The Jam had never sounded as soft, from the chiming guitar to the soft, purring (!) backing harmonies and the tender, first person lyrics. A U.S. single version added around 15 seconds at the end.

HERE COMES THE WEEKEND

'The Weekend Starts Here' was the famous slogan that had kicked off that celebrated mid-Sixties music show, *Ready, Steady, Go!* Weller borrowed the idea for this paean to working life and its two days of weekly freedom.

His opening gambit was insensitive, to say the least: "If we tell you that you got two days to live/Then don't complain 'cause that's one more that you'd get in Zaire." But the song's rousing melody suited its theme – and the line about "score what I need" was one of Paul's few lyrical references to drugs.

TONIGHT AT NOON

Despite being credited solely to Paul Weller, 'Tonight At Noon' took its name from one of Adrian Henri's poems and the first two-and-a-half verses from another, 'In The Midnight Hour'. Both were published in Penguin's best-selling

1967 collection, *The Mersey Sound*, a logical influence on Weller, bearing in mind his interest in Sixties Liverpool and, perhaps unusually for a working-class lad with few qualifications, a fascination with poetry that harked back to his school days. Weller adapted the poem into another ode to Gill Price, helped by suitable embellishments like handclaps, crooned vocal harmonies and acoustic guitar overdubs.

IN THE MIDNIGHT HOUR

The album ended with a barnstorming cover of Wilson Pickett's mid-Sixties Atlantic soul classic – which coincidentally shared its title with the Adrian Henri poem 'borrowed' by Paul on the album's previous song. A live favourite, this high octane performance was a big improvement on 'Slow Down' on *In The City* – and one of the few occasions Weller played harmonica.

NON-ALBUM SONGS

NEWS OF THE WORLD

Bruce Foxton's only A-side for The Jam felt like a stop-gap single, suggesting that Weller, as their principal tunesmith, was struggling to write new material. Issued in February 1978, 'News Of The World' was the third Jam single to include "world" in its title, suggesting a certain lack of imagination.

The energetic guitar break represented Weller's best fretwork yet, and the song's punchy production was a definite progression from the second LP. The song was catchy enough, and its "Punk rock! Power pop!" overture captured the prevalent mood swing in the music papers, but its attack on tabloid journalism was as two-dimensional as the music. Together with a sleeve photo depicting the band strolling down Carnaby Street and a video shot on top of Battersea Power Station, these images maintained a deliberate link with London but, collectively, they further suggested a band treading water. Sales were correspondingly modest, though the single improved on 'This Is The Modern World' by piercing the Top 30.

AUNTIES AND UNCLES (IMPULSIVE YOUTHS)

The first of two B-sides to 'News Of The World' was this charming, melodic song on which Weller sounded more relaxed than ever. An early demo featured occasional fragments of dialogue in the style of the Small Faces' "mustn't grumble" in 'Lazy Sunday'. Its lyrics suggested a V-sign to those around him, perhaps Paul's way of reacting to parental advice about his intense relationship with Gill.

INNOCENT MAN

Having already tackled insanity, traffic congestion and the press, Bruce then dealt with legal injustices on 'Innocent Man'. The song's central three-chord riff was presumably lifted from The Who's 'Baba O'Riley'.

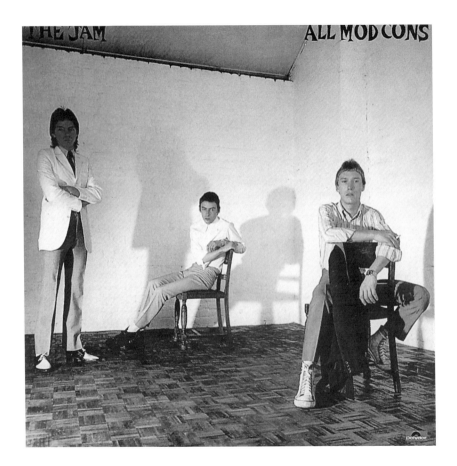

ALL MOD CONS

DATE: NOVEMBER 1978

CHART POSITION: NO. 6

ORIGINAL LP: POLYDOR POLD 5008

CURRENT CD: POLYDOR 537 419-2

By the spring of 1978, Weller's position looked vulnerable. A year into their recording career, The Jam were dogged by internal disputes, troublesome foreign trips and a lead singer, guitarist and principal songwriter who was suffering writer's block.

At the end of the year, their fortunes couldn't have been more different – and the reason was *All Mod Cons*, which not only lodged itself into the Top 10 but was greeted with universal praise by both fans and critics. The Jam had created the first great album to follow punk's two monumental goalposts, *The Clash* and the Sex Pistols' *Never Mind The Bollocks*. In short, *All Mod Cons* was a classic.

In late '77, Weller promised that "for the next LP, I'll have it like a play, with different people singing the lyrics so that everybody will understand". But when he went into the studio in April/May '78, he had just a few rough prototypes, some of which had been written the month before in America. Disenchanted, The Jam rehearsed the new material, but their heart wasn't in it. Producer Chris Parry's derogatory views on these lacklustre demos eventually halted proceedings, and the sessions were aborted. On 1st June, during a concert at London's Paris Theatre for the BBC's 'In Concert' series, the band introduced 'Billy Hunt' as "our new single, out shortly". But it, too, was scrapped. Instead, Weller returned to Woking and the safe surroundings of his parents. With only a week-long tour in early June to disturb him, he pondered The Jam's future.

Up against it, he set about perfecting a batch of tunes that are among the finest of his whole career. "I didn't have a chance to sit around playing them for a long time," he later admitted. "There was a feeling we were being written off. And that spurred me into writing *All Mod Cons*. It was me proving myself."

The turnaround began in August '78 with a song salvaged from the wreckage of those abandoned 'third album' sessions: the punky ' 'A' Bomb In Wardour Street', coupled with The Kinks' 'David Watts', both recorded at veteran producer Mickie Most's Rak Studios. But neither track felt like a great leap forward (and The Kinks cover reinforced the suggestion that the band were weak on new material); the single peaked at only No. 25.

The real landmark happened instead on 6th October, with The Jam's sixth single, 'Down In The Tube Station At Midnight'. Suddenly, they were back in the Top 20, with a stroke of genius widely regarded as the band's greatest accomplishment. It paved the way perfectly for *All Mod Cons,* which followed in November.

Many of the album's songs were rooted in the melodic strength, lyrical edge and sharp, yearning pop of mid-period Beatles, and there was even a suggestion of a concept LP. "You could just take a character like Billy Hunt and centre it around him," Weller explained.

All Mod Cons was the first album with which Weller was totally happy – and with good reason. Freed from a straitjacket of punk/new wave clichés and Who riffs, he created an LP rich with ideas and textures. The increased sophistication and breadth of Weller's songs and their intelligent, intricate structure – their poise – was a great leap forward from the band's 1977 sound. His ambition was clear; Paul had even planned to use snatches of dialogue between the songs, hence the "Thanks to the Southend Kids for conversation" credit, but the idea was dropped at the last moment.

As musicians, the band flourished, with a subtlety The Jam rarely repeated. The trio capitalised on their prolonged studio access to create a more refined 'sound': jagged guitar riffs with overdubs and short, sharp solos and a solid but intricate rhythm section. The sessions were helped by the focus of a single producer: Vic Coppersmith-Heaven (alias Vic Smith) remained after Chris Parry was given his marching orders (he retained a co-production credit for two of the album's earliest recorded songs, 'To Be Someone (Didn't We Have A Nice Time)' and 'It's Too Bad'). Out of the ashes of a scrapped third album rose a masterpiece.

ALL MOD CONS

The short, sharp shock of the opening track set the tone for the LP – confrontational and agitated, Weller snapping around the heels of music industry hypocrisy: "Artistic Freedom, do what you want/But just make sure that the money ain't gone/I'll tell you what, I got you sussed." Both on the album and in concert, 'All Mod Cons' segued into the next track, which shared a similar theme.

TO BE SOMEONE (DIDN'T WE HAVE A NICE TIME)

One of the LP's most powerful songs was this masterpiece, built around a staccato riff interspersed with quieter arpeggio passages. Beneath the surface, you could hear traces of The Beatles' 'Taxman', which later influenced 'The Dreams Of Children', 'Liza Radley' and, most blatantly, 'Start!'. Lyrically, 'To Be Someone' concerned a faded rock star, Weller's first acknowledgement of the trappings of fame, a sideways swipe at the fickle, transient nature of the music industry and the myth of the rock'n'roll lifestyle for which he still professes contempt.

It began with his childhood dream: "To be someone must be a wonderful thing/A famous footballer a rock singer/Or a big film star." But reality soon kicked in – "the bread I spend, is like my fame, it's quickly diminished." All that's left is regret ("I realise I should have stuck to my guns"), hollow nostalgia (the sardonic climax, "Didn't we have a nice time") and withdrawal ("I stay confined to my lonely room"). Amen.

MR. CLEAN

This vehicle for one of Paul's strongest invectives shared the same acid tongue as 'To Be Someone', but the venom was directed at a less obvious target. Weller's hatred of the British class system is well documented, but this was his first direct attack on the middle classes and the besuited business commuter – or, more specifically, the hypocrisy in those who climb the social ladder.

The uneasy incongruity of a Woking childhood, where purest stockbroker-belt territory was littered with post-war working-class council estates, might explain the degree of Weller's rage, as he spat: "If you see me in the street, look away/'Cause I don't ever want to catch you looking at me, Mr. Clean/'Cause I hate you and your wife/And If I get the chance, I'll fuck up your life." His voice was either whispered menace or plain aggressive, and the song's confrontational imagery was

sharpened by its gentle pace. Weller grew up on Stanley Road, adjacent to the town centre and the railway station, so he'd have seen hundreds of Mr. Cleans hurrying to "Catch your train in the morning rain".

DAVID WATTS

'David Watts' was the opening highlight of *Something Else By The Kinks* (1967), which Paul had bought during the band's last trip to the States, and told the tale of "that abominable golden school-boy" as a wider metaphor for teenage insecurity. The Jam had recorded the song as a B-side but were swayed by both Chris Parry and Mickie Most to issue the song as the lead track (double-A-sided with ''A' Bomb').

Although The Jam's version worked in concert – it remained a stage favourite – this seemed like pure mimicry on record. Their treatment replaced Ray Davies' subtly sneering tone for the laddish, terrace-like "oi!, oi!" of Foxton and Weller's shared lead vocals. Maybe they were avoiding the homosexual overtones of the original, with its camp delivery and lines like, "he is so gay and fancy free", and the verse about him avoiding girls because of his "pure and noble creed".

The album version of 'David Watts' was a different mix from that on the single, the most obvious difference being the addition of a piano overdub.

ENGLISH ROSE

Contrast the venom of 'Mr. Clean' with the sentimentality of 'English Rose': "I've sailed the seven seas, I've flown the whole blue sky/But I return with haste, to where my love does lie." Accompanied only by acoustic guitar, and the ambient introduction of a ship's foghorn and gently lapping waves, Weller sang this romantic poem – his first solo recording – in a voice so vulnerable it's enough to make you both laugh and cry. Think of 'English Rose' as 'I Need You' after a year's worth of living; and it would have been unthinkable for a 'punk rocker' to have recorded such a tender ballad. It survived purely because of Weller's obvious sincerity – and its beautiful tune.

The song was reputedly added at the last moment – it wasn't listed on the outer or inner sleeves – or maybe Paul borrowed the idea from The Beatles' 'Her Majesty', the unlisted track on *Abbey Road*. 'English Rose' was originally going to accompany Foxton's 'The Night' on the flip of an earlier, rougher recording of 'Billy Hunt' as a single.

Everything But The Girl later recorded 'English Rose' for an *NME* tape; perhaps that's what drew Weller to the pair when they collaborated on stage and, later, on The Style Council's first album.

IN THE CROWD

This milestone for The Jam continued the lyrical train of thought of 'Away From The Numbers' and 'The Combine', with offbeat wordplays straight out of the Lennon songbook. Weller seemed in an existentialist mood as he described the numbing sensation of a throng of people: "And everyone seems just like me, they struggle hard to set themselves free, and they're waiting for the change."

One review summarised the music perfectly: "Undistorted guitar grows fuzzier and fuzzier; the amount of echo increases; the tempo becomes more manic. The shift from pop ballad to psychotic showcase ends in an avalanche of stock psychedelic touches... As reverberation builds on the vocal, the chorus of 'In The Crowd' fades out and 'Away From The Numbers' fades in. A backward guitar solo tops it off, and snippets of conversation emerge from the mix." Another masterpiece.

BILLY HUNT

Side 2 opened with this bullying punk track which echoed the old Jam, abrasive and angry. But this belied the kind of insightful lyric which elevated Weller above his peers, who might have trundled out some sorry, hackneyed yoof anthem. Instead, Weller's 'Billy Hunt' connected with any teenager, who struggled against the pressures of "foreman Bob... he used

to be a sergeant in the RAF."

Faced with life's treadmill, our modern day 'Billy Liar' invented a "magical world, full of strippers and long-legged girls." The last verse said it all: "No-one pushes Billy Hunt around/Well they do, but not for long/'Cause when I get fit and grow bionic arms/The whole world's gonna wish it weren't born."

IT'S TOO BAD

'It's Too Bad' was another love song delivered in the first person, this time about a relationship in its twilight. The pleasant melody shared the regret of lines like: "It's too bad that we had to break up, too much said for us to ever make up". But then, as ever in Weller's songwriting, there was a sting in the tale, as the music dropped a key to match the accusatory tone: "I could say I'm sorry, But that's not the point is it? You want to play your games and you don't mind if I get hurt." One particular guitar passage echoed the descending chorus of The Beatles' 'She Loves You'.

FLY

Weller's close relationship with his girlfriend was reflected by the presence of two lullabies on *All Mod Cons* – 'English Rose' and the beautiful 'Fly'. The lyrics to the latter betrayed his tender age, with lines like "Why am I here and what have I done/I see the answer's place my trust in you." But the song was saved by its melody, which built from a barely audible acoustic guitar intro and mumbled lyrics into a soaring chorus. Quite what Weller meant about "let's fly away into the demimonde" is open to question, though: he may have meant a twilight world but a dictionary definition of 'demimonde' is 'the class of women who had lost social standing because of sexual promiscuity'!

THE PLACE I LOVE

One of the cornerstones of *All Mod Cons* seemed to recall Weller's Woking childhood: "The place I love is overgrown now/With beautiful moss and colourful flowers." But the rest of the song suggested that the place was, in fact, "always in the back of my mind" – a mental retreat from "those who would hurt us". More than a hint of Lennon's 'There's A Place' off *Please Please Me*, then. The song opened with a 'Dr. Robert'-like riff and breezed along with Weller's trademark taut guitar chords, breaking out with organ fills and soaring guitar for typically reactionary phrases such as, "I'm making a stand against the world."

'A' BOMB IN WARDOUR STREET

The stark, staccato style and lyrics of another of Weller's 'London' songs both echoed the harsh fury of early Clash. References to punk hang-out the Vortex and Wardour Street itself punctuated this attack on the escalating violence in the capital, and its explosion from the West End into the home counties and beyond – linked to the bootboy thug element that hijacked punk. The furious bite of the song's "a-p-o-c-a-l-y-p-s-e" climax felt like a blast of fresh air compared with the limited arrangements of the second album. As with 'David Watts', the single was remixed for the album – the drum intro was shortened (the guitars are heard from the first bar), the solo boasted some extra feedback and there was an additional outro.

DOWN IN THE TUBE STATION AT MIDNIGHT

The Jam's most acclaimed composition was a stroke of genius on several levels. The music was more intricate than any-thing Weller had previously written – and a lengthy recording session helped make it their most sophisticated, too. Its biting clarity separated Bruce's distinctive bass line from Weller's guitar, and the deft touches of an intro and outro of ambient train noises and a musical fade-in at the end added poignancy.

A first-person narrative told a witty, unflinching story of inner city violence – though Paul claimed to have dashed it off around the idea of a short play. The story dealt with a commuter attacked while travelling home on the under-ground, followed by his vivid impressions of the assailants, and the final twist – when he realised they had stolen his keys to dish out a similar treatment to his wife.

Weller's skill lay in the minutiae of the song's graphic images, which prompted public disapproval from Radio 1's Tony Blackburn, who commented: "I think it's disgusting the way these punks sing about violence all the time. Why can't they sing about beautiful things like trees and flowers?". Weller reacted by phoning the station, defending the song 'on air' by emphasising its message of anti-violence.

Trivia notes: the phrase 'smiling, beguiling' was borrowed from The Yardbirds' mid-Sixties classic, 'Evil Hearted You', while the design of the lettering for the single sleeve mimicked the logo of the Small Faces' record label, Immediate.

NON-ALBUM SONGS

SO SAD ABOUT US

On the flip of 'Down In The Tube Station' was a poignant, respectful version of the Who classic (from their second LP, 1966's *A Quick One*). A staple of The Jam's early live set, 'So Sad About Us' paid tribute to the passing in September 1978 of drummer Keith Moon, who gazed out from the back sleeve of the single. The song had been part of The Jam's Polydor demo, which is now available on the *Direction, Reaction, Creation* box set.

THE NIGHT

This throwaway Bruce Foxton song was originally slated to appear as one of the B-sides of 'Billy Hunt'. The single was then scrapped and the same recording of the song carried over to follow 'So Sad About Us' on 'Down In The Tube Station At Midnight'. It seems likely, therefore, that this skinny-tied power pop effort was recorded during those abandoned 'third album' sessions.

STRANGE TOWN

The Jam were never strictly an albums band, often bridging the gap between their annual LPs with stray singles. Here, on top of a stomping Northern Soul beat and that clipped rhythm guitar style of Sixties Motown records, Weller returned to a familiar theme: the 'Strange Town' in question represented his continued fascination with London, with its references to A-Z Guide Books and Oxford Street and the city's impersonal, impenetrable nature. But its description of a visitor's sense of alienation and anonymity – "I'm really a spaceman from those UFOs" – may also have reflected Weller's experiences of being away from home while touring, especially his dislike of America.

Both 'Strange Town' and its B-side, 'The Butterfly Collector', were linked by one of Paul's poems, reproduced on the rear sleeve; Weller's interest in prose soon manifested itself as the first of many extra-musical ventures, a publishing company, Riot Stories.

THE BUTTERFLY COLLECTOR

The Jam must have been in their prime if Weller could afford to tuck this mature classic away on a B-side. 'The Butterfly Collector' became one of The Jam's most popular songs but maybe Weller felt unsure about issuing quieter, more contemplative tunes as A-sides – at least, until 'The Bitterest Pill'.

Based loosely on The Kinks' 'Shangri-La', the song had a subtle, low-key atmosphere, particularly on the verses, which built to a rousing chorus. This only emphasised its vicious lyrical snipe at the rock groupie, inspired by a liaison with Sex Pistols cohort, Sue Catwoman. "It's about a girl I used to know during the punk days," Paul admitted, "who used to like to have a piece of everyone. I exaggerated a lot of the song – you have to exaggerate the truth, otherwise people don't get to see it. And I guess the title comes from the John Fowles book, *The Collector*."

Weller sounded acerbic from the off: "So you finally got what you wanted/You achieved your aim by making the walking lame/And when you just can't get any higher/You use your senses to suss out this week's climber/And the small fame that you've acquired has brought you into God's status but to me you're still a collector." The degree of Weller's disdain is baffling, witness: "And you surely must know the thrill between your legs has worn off".

As a song which dealt with the seedier side of the 'rock star' lifestyle, it linked the jaded rocker of 'To Be Someone' with the obsessive female fan of 'Girl On The Phone', which kicked off The Jam's next album, *Setting Sons*.

SETTING SONS

DATE: NOVEMBER 1979

CHART POSITION: NO. 4

ORIGINAL LP: POLYDOR POLD 5028

CURRENT CD: POLYDOR 537 420-2

If there was ever a Jam 'sound', then it was perfected on this LP, with its use of multi-tracked, overdubbed guitars. Beforehand, Weller had gradually been refining their sound, learning how to use their studio time creatively. Thereafter, Paul fought to distance the band's recordings from a unified and identifiable style, mixing and matching the instruments, drawing on diverse musical styles and, eventually, breaking up The Jam to pursue his soul and jazz leanings.

Setting Sons was the start of that process, with the full string orchestration on Bruce's 'Smithers-Jones', but it remains their most unmistakably Jam-like LP. The album was recorded at Virgin's Townhouse Studios in Shepherds Bush, West London, in summer/autumn 1979, in the wake of two non-album singles, 'Strange Town' and 'When You're Young'. Instead of preparing the songs as demos, or being given the chance to refine them on the road, Paul wrote many of the tunes in the studio, knocking them off from the seed of an idea or a lyric one night and presenting complete songs to the band the next day.

The work-in-progress of four songs can be heard on the Jam retrospective, *Extras*. "What's interesting is that the arrangements on those demos – just me on guitar – are almost exactly the same as they ended up on record," Paul later commented. "When we first kicked off, we would always demo the stuff together. And then, as I got more confident as a writer, I took myself more seriously and had more set ideas about what the bass should do – or drums. And this isn't taking away from Rick or

Bruce – they'd stamp their own identity on it. But I wanted to work out the ideas on my own before presenting them."

'The Eton Rifles' previewed the LP in early November. This was a crucial turning point in the band's career as a singles band, peaking at No. 3. *Setting Sons* arrived later that month. Weller had talked of it originating as a concept piece, "about three close mates, who get split up when the civil war occurs: one joins the left, one veers off to the right while the third one doesn't feel any particular affiliation whatsoever. He's the abstainer. After the war's conclusion, three splintered comrades plan to meet up again."

The mates in question, we later learnt, were Paul's co-founder members of The Jam – Steve Brookes and Dave Waller The idea was inspired by a Dave Waller poem-cum-short story, about three characters – a businessman, a revolutionary and someone with left-of-centre political views – who survive a modern-day English civil war. Its observations of the nation's past,

present and future owed much to George Orwell's faintly patriotic vision, portrayed in his essays. A concept LP was a logical step for Weller, bearing in mind that those musicians whom he most admired – Ray Davies, Pete Townshend, Marriott/Lane, Lennon /McCartney – had had similar ambitions at around the same juncture in their careers.

As it transpired, Weller's grand conceptual scheme fell flat because he didn't have time to complete the concept – and the sessions dragged, due in part to Vic Coppersmith-Heaven's laid-back attitude and the band's increasing use of overdubs and other studio facilities. Only a few songs provided snapshots of the *Setting Sons* characters at various stages in their lives, beginning with the youngsters of 'Thick As Thieves'. Next came the adult world of the businessman of 'Burning Sky'; the ambitious, dramatic anti-war epic, 'Little Boy Soldiers'; and the 'Citizen Smith'-styled caricature of 'The Eton Rifles'.

But the concept was graphically illustrated on the front cover: Benjamin Clemens' striking bronze sculpture of three figures, The St. John's Ambulance Bearers, which painted the perfect picture of the solemn, often bleak imagery of Weller's songs. (The ironic use of British iconography on the inner sleeve – a British bulldog and a Union Jack deckchair on Brighton beach – was a bold move which invited misinterpretation, bearing in mind the previous furore surrounding Weller's past comments about voting Tory.) It would be foolish to read too much into *Setting Sons*' theme, but there's a nagging coincidence between the idea of three friends growing apart and the increasingly separate lives of Paul, Bruce and Rick.

Setting Sons was the archetypal Jam record – dynamic, urgent, snappy and energetic – which may be one reason why Weller spent the rest of the group's life-span trying to escape from it. "I thought *Setting Sons* was too slick, too polished," he confessed. "I don't think it's a really true sound."

GIRL ON THE PHONE

"When anyone tries to sum you up," Paul once said, "they think they know what you're about, and they know bits and pieces – but no-one knows what you're about because I don't know myself." That was the motivation for the clipped, snappy 'Girl On The Phone', which hinted at Weller's discomfort with his increasing fame ("She says she knows everything about me"), while taking a sideways swipe at the press.

THICK AS THIEVES

One of the few songs written prior to the recording sessions, 'Thick As Thieves' dealt with the unique bond which exists between friends, bound together by shared experiences and simply being young – and how this bond dissolves as people inevitably drift apart. "But something came along that changes our minds/I don't know what and I don't know why," wrote Weller, "But we seemed to grow up in a flash of time/While we watched our ideals

helplessly unwind". This idea harked back to 'I Got By In Time' in one sense; in another, it's just a chapter in the concept of *Setting Sons*, of three friends growing apart.

This is quintessential Jam – tight, energetic, catchy, Weller's guitar taut at one moment, delivering harsh power chords at others, but always sparring with intricate bass lines, the whole sound building to an explosive climax.

PRIVATE HELL

Searching for inspiration with studio deadlines imminent, Weller had stumbled across an interview with cult Sixties band The Creation in a 1966 edition of *Record Mirror*, which mentioned two of their new songs. One of them, 'Private Hell', gave Paul the title of this song he then wrote in the studio, a bleak tale of a woman's mid-life crisis that began with the words of the other Creation title, 'Closer Than Close'. The Jam had already paid tribute to the band – who rivalled The Who for that winning mid-Sixties formula of pop art imagery, wide-eyed pop songs and sharp, feedback guitar – by illustrating one of their singles on the inner sleeve of *All Mod Cons*.

The brutal music jerks and shudders, with distorted guitar, pounding bass and a quickfire drum pattern, as Weller uses first name terms – Emma, Terry and Edward – à la Ray Davies. But the lyrics are cold and lack sympathy. If the ageing housewife is suffering her own 'Private Hell', then Weller offers no solutions as the song ends claustrophobically with "private hell" repeated, ad infinitum, smothered in reverb.

LITTLE BOY SOLDIERS

Setting Sons' cornerstone was also its most ambitious song. This anti-war statement was delivered in a laconic style typical of Weller at this time, confrontational but sarcastic, an idealist but also a fatalist who seems to lyrically shrug his shoulders about the inevitable: "These days I find that I can't be bothered /These days I find that it's all too much/To pick up a gun and shoot a stranger/But I've got no choice so here I come – war games."

Halfway through, the pace changed into military time, as befitting the song's theme, with cello (courtesy of Bruce Foxton) and timpani drums, building to a vehement attack on the hypocrisy of war "beneath the flag of democracy". Then Weller delivered the final thrust: "Then they send you home in a pine overcoat/With a letter to your mum/Saying find enlcosed one son, one medal and a note to say he won." The sombre climax was drawn out by a single, elongated piano note which faded slowly.

WASTELAND

'Wasteland' was a rewarding, evocative tale of friendship in the face of adversity, the song's summer-pop melody augmented by organ, jangly guitar, a forlorn flute/recorder and Bruce's effective backing vocals.

The lyrics are over-dramatic, maybe, but viewed as the last part of the concept – three friends returning to all that's left of their childhood stomping ground – 'Wasteland' was *Setting Sons'* most charming song, once accurately described as "The Jam's consummate English pop track".

BURNING SKY

'Burning Sky' picked up the story midway through their lives, Weller's loathing of big business expressed in the form of a cool, patronising letter from one friend to another: "We've all grown up and we've got our own lives/And the values that we had once upon a time, seem stupid now/'Cause the rent must be paid and some bonds severed and others made." The lively bass lines and spiky guitar chords were Jam trademarks, the perfect accompaniment to Weller's Orwell-inspired image of a multi-corporate, financial world that's even truer now than in 1979.

SMITHERS-JONES

Bruce Foxton's most accomplished Jam song first appeared as the B-side to 'When You're Young', with a melody which echoed The Who's 'I Can't Reach You' (from 1967's *Sell Out* album). Its

theme of a middle-aged man thrown onto the employment scrap heap by a company he'd served for many years was inspired by the treatment of Bruce's father. The finishing refrain, written by Weller – "Put on the kettle and make some tea" – closely resembled a line from The Kinks' 'Shangri-La', another reference to the song from their 1969 LP, *Arthur*. With a studio deadline for *Setting Sons* looming, Rick Buckler suggested they re-record 'Smithers-Jones' with a twenty-piece orchestra – the 'Jam Philharmonic', as they were billed.

SATURDAY'S KIDS

Chosen as a single in America, 'Saturday's Kids' was another song written about the crowd of friends with whom Weller grew up in Woking, with references to the 'Lite-A-Bite' and his regular holiday haunts of Selsey Bill and nearby Bracklesham Bay. The song's theme echoed that of 'In The Crowd', only the images here were far more direct: "Saturday's kids live in council houses, Wear V-necked shirts and baggy trousers/Drive Cortinas, fur-trimmed dashboards, Stains on the seats – in the back of course!" And "dip in silver paper when you're pint's gone flat" was another reference to drugs: Weller has since admitted to a fondness for 'speed' during his youth.

'Saturday's Kids' was a clever picture of suburban teenage life littered with incisive references which anyone might relate to, expanded from a poem which had originally joined several of Paul's literary efforts in the back of an *All Mod Cons* songbook. "It's a documentation of that lifestyle," Weller later commented. "It was actually written about my schoolfriends – all the people who still go down my local pub."

THE ETON RIFLES

The Jam's breakthrough hit was introduced by a barrage of dissonant guitar and thundering bass, before settling down into one of their accepted classics – anthemic, aggressive and venomous but also melodic. The song was based around a repetitive, quickfire bass line,

allowing Weller to rip atonal chords out of his guitar (especially on the album version, which is noticeably longer than the single), though the aggressive mood was lightened in the middle by an organ solo.

"I saw this TV programme and thought it was a good title," said Paul. "But the actual song is just a piss-take of the class system. I'm a very class conscious person. I realise it's a joke and it shouldn't really exist in the 1980s but it still does. It's also a piss-take of these trendy socialists and fascists." The song's message was later underlined by the behaviour of some Eton schoolboys, who taunted demonstrators on one of the numerous 'Right To Work' marches against rising unemployment.

HEATWAVE

A hectic barroom cover of this live Jam favourite was tagged on the end on *Setting Sons*, a last-minute decision due to their impending deadline. 'Heatwave' was the Martha & the Vandellas' Motown classic from 1964 (as covered by The Who). But this finale seemed to emphasise a dearth of new songs and sounded a hurried, despite guest appearances from Mick Talbot (of mod revivalists the Merton Parkas) on piano and Rudi on sax. Talbot also guested at some of The Jam's London concerts, before eventually reuniting with Paul in The Style Council.

NON-ALBUM SONGS

WHEN YOU'RE YOUNG

This punchy dose of social realism à la The Who's 'My Generation' combined Weller's continued obsession over the spirit of youth with a growing cynicism and disillusionment. It was crystallised by the line, "The world is your oyster, but your future's your clam", a poignant lyric from the first Jam single to be released after the Conservatives' election victory in May 1979. Musically, 'When You're Young' was classic, stock-in-trade Jam, a spiky sound which bordered on the anthemic, that was radio-friendly but jagged enough to

separate it from slicker new wave offspring like The Police and The Pretenders.

SEE-SAW

Paul had originally given the sprightly B-side of 'The Eton Rifles' to Glasgow band and fellow Polydor act The Jolt, who had been actively encouraged to follow in The Jam's wake. Their version of 'See Saw' had graced their *Maybe Tonight* EP in early 1979.

GOING UNDERGROUND

'Going Underground' was the culmination of everything The Jam had strived for since their days at the Woking Working Men's Club back in the mid-Seventies. Its anthemic chorus was guaranteed to gel with the band's loyal fanbase, while a witty and effective lyric made reference to the atomic bomb, an all-too-real threat after Russia's invasion of Afghanistan in December '79 – though the song's lyrics also suggested a nihilistic rejection of society.

Polydor devised a useful marketing

incentive: a double-pack single adding live tracks. With 200,000 advance orders, the single was guaranteed to enter the charts at No. 1 (especially after its release was 'delayed' for a week because of a supposed pressing problem), the first time this had happened since Slade's 'Merry Xmas Everybody' in 1973. "Near to tears when 'Going Underground' goes to the top!", was how Paul later expressed his reaction on the sleeve of *Dig The New Breed*.

THE DREAMS OF CHILDREN

'Going Underground' had been planned as a double-A-side, coupled with this more experimental track, which mined the same faintly psychedelic seam and oblique lyrics of earlier songs like 'In The Crowd'. The intro was taken from an earlier song, 'Thick As Thieves'. "When we finished off *Setting Sons*," Paul explained, "I got the engineer to play the album backwards and there was just one little piece of backward vocal I liked. 'The Dreams Of Children' was built around that, more-or-less made up on the spot." The technique reflected Paul's growing love of British psychedelia, especially '66-era Beatles and early Pink Floyd ("I'll tell you a guitarist I really do like and that's Syd Barrett," Paul proffered in 1981).

SOUND AFFECTS

DATE: NOVEMBER 1980
CHART POSITION: NO. 2
ORIGINAL LP: POLYDOR POLD 5035
CURRENT CD: POLYDOR 537 421-2

Sound Affects was The Jam's *Revolver*. Indeed, the Beatles' album was stamped all over Paul's songs, from guitar riffs and basslines to the stark, proto-psychedelic production – partly because it had been on permanent rotation on The Jam's tour bus during their last American visit. *Sound Affects* also remains their most challenging album — and Paul's favourite, to this day.

In the wake of the No. 1 success of 'Going Underground', the band worked on their next album throughout summer 1980 – again at Townhouse Studios. While they were in Japan, a row ensued over their next single. Paul wanted 'Start!' but Polydor preferred another, more typical new song, 'Pretty Green'. Eventually, Polydor relented, and The Jam notched up their second consecutive No. 1 in August.

The Jam's fifth LP followed in late November – but not before more arguments with Polydor. Weller hadn't wanted to finish the album until the new year because he didn't have enough songs. But the record label weren't having a great financial year, and made the bizarre suggestion that The Jam's principal songwriter work with Godley & Creme. Eventually, Weller was forced – as with *Setting Sons* – to knock up new material at short notice.

The album was named after a BBC *Sound Effects* record Weller found lying around the studio, which also inspired the striking pop-art sleeve, each photo linked to a lyric on the album. The subtle title change ("Effects" to "Affects") switched the emphasis from passive to active. "It's in the lyrics of 'Start!' as well", Paul explained, emphasising his view of the potential power of music.

Sound Affects was an album of peaks and troughs rather than one of consistency. In contrast to *Setting Sons*, its edgy, claustrophobic atmosphere was influenced by the atonal style of post-punk acts like Wire, Gang Of Four and Joy Division – excepting the odd funk bassline and acoustic track. Weller summed up the mood change: "I was drunk one night at The Venue, and someone said, 'What's the album sound like?' And I replied, a mixture between *Revolver* and Michael Jackson's *Off The Wall*."

Another source of inspiration was Geoffrey Ashe's *Camelot And The Vision Of Albion*. The idea that "we had lost sight of our purpose and our goal as human beings, that material goals had hidden our spiritual ones and clouded our perception" ran through much of the album. Another was George Orwell's story of fighting against fascism, *Homage To Catalonia*, which reflected the author's growing interest in democratic socialism. Paul's songwriting was clearly in a state of transition.

Sound Affects may be Weller's favourite Jam album today, but at the time he wasn't happy with Vic Coppersmith-Heaven's flat production, nor the producer's slow, laborious methods. The album had to be recut on numerous occasions in an attempt to compensate for the disappointment of the final masters and it was the last time Coppersmith-Heaven worked with The Jam.

The 1980 end-of-year readers' polls confirmed The Jam as the most popular contemporary band in Britain. In one survey, they won best 'group', 'male singer', 'guitarist', 'bass', 'drums', 'songwriter', 'single', 'album' and 'cover art'. Despite the band's reservations, *Sound Affects* sold over 100,000 copies and would have topped the charts had it not been for Abba's *Super Trouper*.

PRETTY GREEN

This militant album opener began with a thundering one-note bass-line, which underpinned the whole song, as Weller launched into a caustic attack on society in which "power is measured by the pound or the fist". 'Pretty Green' had a brittle, tense air, setting the scene for another bleak outlook on society; in fact, *Sound Affects* was no more optimistic than *Setting Sons*. Weller adopted a deliberately simplistic view of a society ruled by money: "I've got a pocket full of pretty green... I'm going to give it the man behind the counter/He's going to give me food and water."

An early demo was included on a cassette free with *Select* magazine, though a more radical acoustic prototype can now he heard on *Direction, Reaction, Creation.*

MONDAY

'Monday' was less obviously Jam-like, Weller's poetic lyrics delivered deadpan above an atmospheric, almost psychedelic tune. "I will never be

embarrassed about love again", cries the singer, before the song takes a turn. "Tortured winds that blew me over/When I start to think I'm something special/They tell me that I'm not/And they're right and I'm glad I'm not." The music is simplicity itself, drifting along with a loping bass line and brash, trebly guitar stabs, its ethereal melody helped along by ghostly backing vocals.

BUT I'M DIFFERENT NOW

One of the more traditional tracks on *Sound Affects* was built around a staccato guitar riff reminiscent of another *Revolver* song, 'Dr. Robert'. The barely decipherable lyrics trod a well-worn path for Weller – a love song tinged with regret – summed up by this simple message: "I know I've done some things which I should never have done/But I'm different now and I'm glad that you're my girl." A middle eight recalled Talking Heads (much to Weller's later chagrin), while the central riff got a different twist before the song ended abruptly, clocking in at under two minutes.

SET THE HOUSE ABLAZE

If Weller felt a growing conviction about the injustices of society, then he also seemed frustrated by his own inability to change them. "I wish that there was something I could do about it", he maligned in 'Set The House Ablaze', a title which mirrored the revolutionary theme of the poem on the back sleeve, 'Mask Of Anarchy' by Percy Bysshe Shelley.

Some disarmingly jolly whistling accompanied the song's opening, repetitive guitar motif, before the lyrics suggested a feeling of general despair.

START!

Originally entitled 'Two Minutes' (from the line, "If we get through for two minutes only/It will be a start!"), The Jam's second No. 1 dealt with the importance of human contact, and whether that could be achieved through a pop record. Critics focused instead on the song's musical debt to 'Taxman' from *Revolver*. Its stripped-to-the-bone production, the bass riff and the harsh, trebly guitar

(especially the whining, backwards-sounding solo), were patently lifted from George Harrison's proto-psychedelic album opener. But Weller was defensive about the accusations of plagiarism: "Apart from the first notes, the rest of the bass line is quite different," he countered, and has since added that listeners weren't meant not to notice the resemblance between the songs. 'Start!' was then remixed for the album.

THAT'S ENTERTAINMENT

'That's Entertainment' is perhaps Weller's most vivid snapshot of English life. Its sardonic title and gritty images of everyday life painted a depressing picture of a decaying Britain, using direct language which mixed the suburban boredom of 'Saturday's Kids' with the urban commentary of 'Tube Station'. The song was heralded as a masterpiece, much to the bemusement of its author, who claimed to have dashed it off after returning from the pub one night. In fact, the core theme was based on a poem, 'Entertainment', which had appeared in one of Weller's *Riot Stories* publications, suggesting a certain degree of plagiarism on Paul's part.

The Jam resisted the temptation to issue 'That's Entertainment' as the follow-up to 'Start!' But when the song was chosen as a single in Germany, it became Britain's best-selling import single to date. It's a telling indication of the song's encapsulation of British life that 'That's Entertainment' was later covered by two quintessentially English acts, Morrissey and the Wonder Stuff.

DREAM TIME

Based around another of Paul's poems, this excellent track might best be described as psychedelic punk. The music begins with a quiet backwards guitar intro, which slowly fades in, accompanied only by some ethereal backing vocals. Then the song proper crashes in quite suddenly, Weller delivering an existential view of the world, picking up where 'In The Crowd' left off before stating that "It's a tough, tough world /But you've got to be tough to bear it".

MAN IN THE CORNER SHOP

No less sublime was 'Man In The Corner Shop', which starts as a tale of ordinary folk, and how the grass always appears to be greener in other people's lives. But there are deeper thoughts at work here, dealing with aspects of human nature like hardship, jealousy and inequality. The melody, which Weller invented to order in the studio, has a sad quality which complements the mournful nature of the lyrics.

The song has been described as an "agnostic religious ode", principally because of the closing lines, the last of which is repeated, anthem-like: "Go to church do the people from the area/All shapes and classes sit and pray together/For here they are all one/For God created all men equal."

(On the edge of the Maybury Estate in Woking, where the Wellers moved in 1976, a corner shop lies opposite a factory on the main road; this locale has been suggested as the inspiration for the song.)

MUSIC FOR THE LAST COUPLE

The Jam's first group composition must rank as one of The Jam's most offbeat offerings. For 30 seconds or so, the music consist only of odd, abstract rhythmic noises (probably inspired by Syd Barrett's quirky creation, 'The Scarecrow', from Pink Floyd's first album, *The Piper At The Gates Of Dawn*). A fly buzzes quietly as random bass noises disturb the peace. And nothing's much clearer once the music starts, from the oompah drum beat to Weller's scratchy guitar (which often reverts to a chopped ska feel), the skewed horns and what sounds like a melodia impersonating a car horn. The only lyrics to speak of are no less unsettling: "I think of boats and trains and all those things/That make you want to get away."

BOY ABOUT TOWN

Such was the stark, intimate nature of much of *Sound Affects* that the bright and breezy 'Boy About Town' sounds almost rude. This punchy mod anthem barges along, helped by a horn section and a melody that was written to be whistled. The opening lines, "See me walking around, I'm the boy about town that you've heard of", recalled Ray Davies' Swinging Sixties images of 'Dandy' and 'Dedicated Follower Of Fashion', but the rest of the song is quite poetic.

The idea was probably inspired by a free London commuter magazine of the time, *Girl About Town*. Another of Paul's 'London' tributes, then: "It's just me being blown about up and down Oxford Street," he commented. A rougher version of the song appeared on a flexidisc free with *Flexipop* magazine.

SCRAPE AWAY

"Your twisted cynicism makes me feel sick... You've given up hope, you're jaded and ill... You're all dried up and don't believe": Weller may have felt impotent about his ability to change what he saw as social injustices but *Sound Affects'* closing gambit attacked the decline in people's ideals as they age. It's been suggested that he was decrying those third generation punks, but their empty nihilism and clichéd cries for chaos were only part of the equation. The music is equally bleak, from Foxton's cyclical, four-note bass riff to the verbal soap box rant (singing would be too strong a description), culminating in the mantra, "You who's scraping away", as the music is pared back to the bare bones of that bass line. French dialogue fades in, creating a psychedelic aura, while the gritty guitar momentarily exudes feedback.

NON-ALBUM SONGS

LIZA RADLEY

'Start!' was backed by one of Paul's last 'character' songs, which he later described as "me playing around and just being quasi-psychedelic or a bit Syd Barrett, a piece of English whimsy." Weller strummed acoustic guitar, plucked some overdubs and sang a forlorn tale of "Liza Radley, see the girl with long hair", who creeps "across summer lawns at midnight", who'll "kiss my face and say 'life means nothing at all'." It was all very 'Norwegian Wood', right down to Bruce's accordion, while the bass pattern was disarmingly similar to 'Start!'.

POP-ART POEM

Originally known as 'Go Native', this clever DIY collage of psychedelic effects was coupled with a demo of 'Boy About Town' on a *Flexipop* flexidisc in autumn 1980. Weller is heard mumbling snatches of words, set to a murky, other-worldly accompaniment. The deadpan prose was based around a poem written for his *December Child* fanzine: "I played all the instruments on it. They're all slowed down and speeded up to get that weird effect. It was restricted to the flexi because I didn't know how The Jam's audience would have felt about it." Taped while the band were completing *Sound Affects* in September 1980, 'Pop-Art Poem' is now available on *Extras*.

FUNERAL PYRE

1981 was The Jam's quietest year for records – partly because Weller struggled to maintain (or wanted to escape) their previous pattern of issuing an album per year. Their frontman was also becoming increasingly disillusioned with pop's shift towards a more lightweight, synth sound, where fancy haircuts mattered more than lyrics.

Weller reacted by creating The Jam's most uncompromising musical statement. Issued in May 1981, 'Funeral Pyre' was a fiery, discordant single – and their first to be produced by engineer Pete

Wilson, who had grown increasingly involved with the band during the recording of *Sound Affects*.

The lyrics' colourful metaphor attacked what Weller perceived as the hate and greed among those in power, powerfully communicated by brutal guitar and Rick Buckler's persistent drum rolls. The glimmer of a tune had to fight its way from beneath a sea of distortion. "To have a hit that didn't have a pretty guitar phrase or a chorus represented what we sounded like live," Paul explained. "I was conscious that we might get too pop, especially when we started having No. 1s. A lot of groups go the whole way and get more diluted. I wanted to make sure we go the other way and maintain our popularity but not choose the easy route."

The single stalled at No. 4, a modest reflection of The Jam's enormous popularity. But coming after their longest-ever break between singles, and carrying a writing credit that read, 'Words: Paul Weller, Music: The Jam', 'Funeral Pyre' suggested disquiet within the band.

DISGUISES

'Disguises' was an obscure Who song which had been tucked away on their *Ready Steady Who* EP in 1966. The song had an other-worldly, near-psychedelic quality, and in this respect, The Jam's version picked up where *Sound Affects* left off. Weller took a leaf from Pete Townshend's effects-laden guitar sound to create a fractured wall of sound far harsher than The Who's, burying the song's pleasant melody under a howl of strung-out treble. "I had this bootleg of Pete Townshend demos and he did 'Disguises'," Paul later revealed. "We took the cue from that, since the mix was fucking awful on *Ready Steady Who.*"

ABSOLUTE BEGINNERS

Weller's first attempt at integrating funk into The Jam's rather rigid style wasn't a great success. Issued as a single in October 1981, 'Absolute Beginners' was a clumsy, disjointed collision of horns, guitar and an uncomfortable rhythm section. It masked the mystical, if somewhat pretentious lyrics, of a genuinely charming song, which took its title from Colin MacInnes' quintessential novel about late Fifties London, whose central character embodied the Modernist lifestyle of jazz, clean living, independence and scooters – in roughly that order (though Weller had yet to read the book). The song had provisionally been entitled 'Skirt' – though the reason why has remained a mystery.

TALES FROM THE RIVERBANK

From *Sound Affects* onwards, The Jam's music was less direct, less in-your-face. It kept its bite but some songs had a less tangible mood. 'Tales From The Riverbank' was a case in point, one of The Jam's most beguiling creations and one of the strongest, most enduring songs Weller has ever written. 'Riverbank' found Weller waxing lyrical around a theme of his Woking childhood in the surrounding Surrey countryside. The swirling music, full of layered guitar and quirky piano, created

a spooky psychedelic vibe. The track would have made a wonderful A-side – in fact, Weller has openly regretted its relegation to the flip of 'Absolute Beginners' ever since. The song had grown out of two earlier prototypes, 'Not Far At All' and the more frantic 'We've Only Started' (which finally surfaced on *Extras*).

An alternate version was sent out as a flexidisc to fan club members early in 1982. "It's a re-recorded version we did originally for the LP, *The Gift*," wrote Paul in the accompanying letter. "The main difference is the added brass, which is how we've been doing it live." The Jam had just added a horn section, further confirmation of Weller's wish to create a more soulful sound.

In 1998, Paul flew in the face of previously shunning his past by re-recording 'Riverbank' for his only new single of that year, 'Brand New Start' (an ironic title, then), retaining the song's melancholic flavour while altering some of the original lyrics.

THE JAM ★ THE GIFT

THE GIFT

DATE: MARCH 1982

CHART POSITION: NO. 1

ORIGINAL LP: POLYDOR POLD 5055

CURRENT CD: POLYDOR 537 422-2

In late 1981, Paul Weller publicly vowed to make the group's next LP their best-ever. In the process, he suffered a minor nervous breakdown, fell out with members of the band and wrote some of his most moving songs. But it was also the start of the end of The Jam.

The Gift is one of the least satisfying Jam LPs, perhaps because it sounds forced. After the sense of impotence expressed in the lyrics of *Setting Sons* and *Sound Affects*, Weller now saw a way forward. The Jam's pulling power could be harnessed for direct action: to focus awareness on specific political issues while also raising proceeds for those causes. Weller's troubled conscience and pent-up frustration were given a release valve, although he was cautious about aligning himself with left-wing campaigns, en masse, despite his growing socialist convictions.

In late 1981, The Jam started recording with new producer Pete Wilson in Oxford Street's AIR London Studios, owned by ex-Beatles producer George Martin. The sessions were split into two halves. "I wrote the rest of the tracks over Christmas," Paul explained. "I came back with about six songs I'd finished at home." Driven to develop beyond The Jam's orthodox rock sound, he worked hard during the day and played hard by night, absorbing London's nightlife and reflecting its influence in his music. Weighed down by the sole songwriting responsibilities, Weller gagged under the weight of expectation. A gulf widened between him and the other members, and tensions rose in the studio. Something had to give; taking a break from the sessions one day, Weller collapsed at a pool table, suffering what was described as a mini-breakdown.

Nevertheless, The Jam's return in early February 1982 was triumphant. The double-A-sided 'Town Called Malice' / 'Precious' was the band's second single to enter the charts at No. 1. Both songs were performed back-to-back on *Top Of The Pops,* a feat not seen since The Beatles' 'We Can Work It Out' / 'Day Tripper'; and both successfully integrated black influences into The Jam's sound.

Both also appeared on *The Gift,* issued that March. An uncompromising stance was revealed in the lyrics of many of its songs, especially the key tracks, which ended each side ('The Gift', ' "Trans-Global Express"). These led a tirade against those in power – the ruling classes, heads of state, industrial bosses – and their effects on the less privileged. "The general statement to come out the LP," explained Paul, "is a call for unity amongst working-class people." This may have been an ironic,

idealistic quest, bearing in mind the fraying relationships within the band.

"The overall sound/effect is quite soul-influenced," said Weller of the LP, "but not necessarily Tamla Motown, like Elvis [Costello] did with *Get Happy.* I wanted to create a 1980s brand of soul." Hence the addition of saxophonist Keith Thomas and trumpeter Steve Nichol. The album's packaging, as ever, was ingenious; the album was sold in a striped pink 'gift' bag, featuring a photo of a Northern Soul dancer on the inner sleeve.

There was no doubting Paul's efforts or intentions – moreover, his voice had improved, adding more range to his vocals. But in trying to forge a new vision for The Jam, the album felt incomplete and a little patchy. Weller occasionally sounded pretentious and affected – and despite the talk of soul, The Jam still sounded like a rock band. Despite the conversational style of the album's lyrics, few songs broadcast their views accessibly. Weller disagreed: "I think it's the best thing we've ever done. The lyrics are really simple, more conversational. I think that's the best way to get across exactly what I feel. It's probably our most diverse LP and I put everything I've got into it."

HAPPY TOGETHER

Bearing in mind growing tensions within The Jam, there was a hollow ring about the title of the album's opener, one of the genuine masterpieces on an otherwise disjointed affair. Somehow, Weller captured the sense of passion he was striving for, and the song motored along to a strident Northern Soul beat. Weller's lyrics to 'Happy Together' were both loving and sarcastic, perhaps reflecting a volatile stage in his relationship with his girlfriend.

GHOSTS

"All of us, including me, try to disguise ourselves with clothes or different attitudes," said Weller, describing the most beautiful song on *The Gift*. "There's this weakness in most people. Look at all these cults. People darting around into different sets of clothes. There just seems to be something missing. Either we don't want to face up to our own individuality or we're frightened of what we might find."

'Ghosts', then, dealt with facing up to yourself. "Why are you frightened, can't you see that it's you," crooned Weller, "That ain't no ghost, it's a reflection of you/Why do you turn away, an' keep it out of sight". Like 'Happy Together', the song was composed in the studio, and boasted a subtlety, ranging from Buckler's 'rim-shot' drumming to the sparring horns, which The Jam rarely achieved elsewhere.

PRECIOUS

If 'Town Called Malice' echoed mid-Sixties soul, then 'Precious' acknowledged Seventies funk – classics like Brass Construction's 'Movin' ' – with a respectful nod towards Pigbag's contemporary hit, 'Papa's Got A Brand New Pigbag'. The poetical lyrics were underscored by Paul's rhythmic wah-wah guitar and the stabbing horn riffs of new arrivals Steve Thomas and Keith Nichol. Three studio variations exist: the edited 7", the elongated album version and, longest of all, the extended 12" mix.

"I wasn't 100 per cent for releasing this as a single," commented Weller, "because I thought people would think we were jumping on the white funk thing. I just wanted to write an updated version of early Seventies soul. 'Precious' is a love song, written directly about me."

JUST WHO IS THE FIVE O'CLOCK HERO?

This a ironic yet sympathetic tale of the "constant struggle just to exist" was strong enough to make the Top 10 as an import single, affirming it as one of the album's highlights. Weller returned to the 'character' technique of *All Mod Cons* and *Setting Sons* – and its pessimism, too, was out of kilter with Weller's self-confessed "new optimism". Paul had rarely dealt directly with specific political issues, but now he concentrated his vitriol on the class system, the inhumanities of big business – and his support for CND. 'Five O'Clock Hero' didn't pull any punches: "My hard earned dough goes in bills and the larder/And that Prince Philip tells us we've got to work harder!" It was the next rung up a politically aware ladder that led the singer to the outright lyrical attacks of The Style Council.

"The real heroes are obviously the geezer who has to go out and do a nine-to-five job," said Weller – who'd never done a normal day's work in his life. "Those images are already with me... The nurses and miners are the real heroes because they keep the country going – not pop stars."

"TRANS-GLOBAL EXPRESS"

This riotous semi-instrumental stole the riff from the World Column's funky Northern Soul classic, 'So Is The Sun', warped into a cacophony using psychedelic and dub techniques. The title was borrowed from the name of an old railway company, which Kraftwerk had also adapted for an album, while the "oink! oink!" sounds at the start were inspired by reggae stars Clint Eastwood & General Saint.

You had to read the words to understand the song's message: a revolutionary call-to-arms to "see the hands of oppression fumble, and their systems crash to the ground". The song also attacked Weller's peers: "It was my anti- Sting rap: 'we can't change nothing, there's no political solution, we're all weaklings, let's give up and commit suicide'. Those people make me sick – if I believed there was no political situation, I'd slash my wrists. The song's optimistic. The ideas come from travelling around, meeting people from other countries and realising everyone has the same problems."

Weller's most poignant lyrics were kept till last: "The day the working people join together we'll all rest much more easy/And the responsibility that you must bear when it's your own future in your own hands/May be a hard one to face up to/But at least you'll own yourself."

RUNNING ON THE SPOT

'Running On The Spot' was classically upbeat Jam, though its ringing guitar riff and ingenious production remoulded their musical shape, with some excellent backing harmonies towards the end. The song's message was embodied by the line: "Stop revelling in rejection".

CIRCUS

Bruce Foxton's clumsy funk instrumental was as unimaginative as its title, chosen because AIR London's studio overlooked Piccadilly Circus. 'Circus' – Like 'Precious' – was indebted to Pigbag's mix of percussive funk and simple horn riffs.

"Bruce came up with the main riff," Weller remembered. "We all put stuff in but the basic idea is his. It works more than things on *Sound Affects*, a little light relief, a dance track." (Talk of a vocal version, with Bananarama of all people, came to nothing.)

THE PLANNER'S DREAM GOES WRONG

One of *The Gift*'s main pitfalls was this attack on rundown high-rise council blocks. The song's appealing melody was spoilt by a jarring attempt at ethnicity, using Caribbean steel drums played by Russ Henderson. Still, the lyrics effectively punctured the myth of "dream life luxury living", an ill-fated urban development plan promised via a "pleasant No. 10 whim" in the Sixties and Seventies. "I was working on cinematic song titles," suggested Weller. "The music is all Notting Hill Gate, party time, but the lyrics are the other side of Notting Hill...

"One architect in particular was commissioned in the early Sixties to design those tower blocks, but I don't suppose he ever lived in them. That's the story of British society. It's controlled and planned by the rich classes."

CARNATION

'Carnation' offered one of the most charming tunes on the album, disguising lyrics which dealt with greed and avarice. "It's about mono vision and the one-dimensional idea of capitalism," Paul explained. "It's okay for people who are getting the money, but other people have to earn it for them. You're born and your sole purpose is to go through school, get the best job – in many cases, the one that pays the most – and if you're lucky, you work until you're 65, then they put you out to graze until you peg it. There's got to be more to it than that."

Was there a deeper, more spiritual side to Weller's character? "I don't belong to any particular religion, but I do believe in God as such. 'Carnation' is a symbol of something fresh and growing and the way that anything with colour or imagination is snubbed out."

TOWN CALLED MALICE

Against a Tamla Motown backdrop, 'Town Called Malice' was another superb slice of social realism. Following on from songs like 'Private Hell' and 'That's Entertainment', Weller questioned the mundanity of life's day-to-day chores by creating vivid images of "lonely housewives", "disused milk floats" and "Sunday's roast beef" – stylistically similar to the poems of Dave Waller and Aidan Cant, published by *Riot Stories*.

Weller has since sounded suprisingly critical of this famous Jam song: "This has the weakest lyrics, from a personal point of view. It doesn't come up to the standards of the other songs. I always wanted to do a song with that Motown beat, like Madness did with 'Embarrassment'. I'm influenced by Aidan quite a lot. I like those lonely suburban images. The main crux of the song is: 'I'd rather put some joy back in this town called malice'. I didn't expect it to be No. 1."

THE GIFT

The title track had an evangelical lyric concerning "the gift of life", and a together-we-can-be-strong message which brought to mind the uplifting, spiritual tones of socially minded early Seventies soul. Its guitar riff was lifted from an obscure Small Faces track, 'Don't Burst My Bubble', but the worthwhile lyrics were sadly buried beneath a murky production.

Weller expanded on its theme, which was central to the album: "I don't hate the rich classes but if they're into the idea of a universal world, then quit your corporations. I don't wish anyone any violence, but hand them over to the people who they rightfully belong to." The last song The Jam ever played live was 'The Gift' – it was a poignant finish.

NON-ALBUM SONGS

THE GREAT DEPRESSION

The German import single for 'The Planner's Dream Goes Wrong' was joined by two songs recorded at Maison Rouge Studios in Fulham in early 1982. The first was 'The Great Depression', with its savage lyric matched to a lilting melody, which shared the same loose feel as the A-side. This might have made a more satisfactory single than 'The Bitterest Pill': Rick Buckler's offbeat, clip-clop drumming, the song's crisp production, and the carefree nature of the chorus only emphasised its anti-Thatcher generation lyrics. Lines like "I'm alright so sod the rest in the new dissension", were married to a breezy horn section. "The song was good and the melody was great," agreed Paul. "But it was the first track we tried to produce ourselves, which is probably why it came out really badly!"

WAR

The Jam's rousing treatment of 'War' reworked Edwin Starr's 1970 Motown classic. Tucked away on the 12" import of 'The Planner's Dream Goes Wrong', the song had initially been slated for a cover versions EP. A more radical version, recorded later that year with backing vocalists Afrodiziak, appeared on the bonus disc of The Jam's swansong single, 'Beat Surrender'.

THE BITTEREST PILL (I EVER HAD TO SWALLOW)

Also recorded at Maison Rouge was this lush ballad – an ironic title, bearing in mind that Weller told the other Jam members of his intention to finish the band during sessions for the single in June/July.

When 'The Bitterest Pill (I Ever Had To Swallow)' finally arrived in early September, Paul's sense of humour was lost on many fans. How could The Jam create such a straightforward pop song – with ornate string accompaniment,

too? The song echoed the big Sixties productions of singers like Dusty Springfield (indeed, an out-take on the Jam box set contains a very Sixties-ish break), but sounded hollow and Weller's voice sounded uncomfortable.

It's also tempting to sympathise with Foxton's complaint that "it was just becoming the Paul Weller show". Weller was friendly with The Belle Stars' Jenny McKeown, who sang backing vocals on the single. Department S vocalist Vaughn Toulouse posed on the single's front cover; and Vaughn's friend, Lee Kavanagh was seen kissing Paul in the video. Maybe, in hindsight, 'The Bitterest Pill' was the first Style Council single – only it was credited to The Jam.

PITY POOR ALFIE–FEVER

Flipping 'The Bitterest Pill' over, 'Pity Poor Alfie' might have pointed a way forward for The Jam. Crashing in with horns, the song's groovy, swinging vibe brought to mind the theme tune to Britain's best-loved Seventies cop series, *The Sweeney*. It then segued into 'Fever', Little Willie John's R&B classic popularised in 1958 by Peggy Lee's jazz-pop hit. The box set belatedly revealed that 'Pity Poor Alfie' had started life as a funk workout more in keeping with Weller's later experiments with The Style Council.

BEAT SURRENDER

Details of a farewell Jam single swiftly followed the announcement of their split – but behind the scenes, Paul hadn't been able to decide between 'Beat Surrender' and a title already familiar to Jam fans as the banner from their previous tour, 'Solid Bond In Your Heart'. Eventually, the latter was saved for Weller's next band, The Style Council.

Issued in late November, 'Beat Surrender' was guaranteed to top the charts, giving them their third single to début at No. 1. Reflecting Weller's growing infatuation with old Stax and Motown, the song's Northern Soul beat was introduced by a piano riff, with a yearning melody and an anthemic chorus. The guitar was conspicuous by its absence. Instead, piano and horns were in the driving seat, which set the template for Weller's future musical endeavour.

On the front sleeve, Gill Price reflected the song's poignant title by modelling with a white flag, while Paul contributed a pretentious sleeve proclamation, with key words highlighted in pop-art colour, under the guise of The Boy Wonder – the first of several sleeve-writing pseudonyms.

SHOPPING

One of the most offbeat Jam creations was this low-key "cod-jazz" B-side to 'Beat Surrender' – an obvious title from the fashion-conscious Weller but actually a laconic look at consumerism. Its deadpan (and off-key) vocals and lazy atmosphere lent themselves to the lyrics: "As I flit from shop window to window and try to pick up a friendly bargain /But it's not like the adverts all make out/And there's no-one to greet you as a friend". 'Shopping' captured Weller's first dabblings with jazz – Rick played with brushes – as the logical progression from 'Pity Poor Alfie-Fever'.

MOVE ON UP

Weller had always indulged his love of Sixties soul ('Back In My Arms Again', 'Slow Down', 'In The Midnight Hour', 'Heatwave'). But by 1982, his taste in black music was widening to encompass Seventies (and early Eighties) soul and funk. Hence this version of Curtis Mayfield's 1971 hit, a classic call to rise above the day-to-day drudgery of the human condition. Having been performed live for nigh on a year, this studio recording finally appeared on the double pack for The Jam's finale, 'Beat Surrender'. It's a respectful treatment – although The Jam couldn't hope to better the original. Weller later resurrected the song with The Style Council.

STONED OUT OF MY MIND

Together with 'Move On Up' and 'War', this respectful tribute to The Chi-Lites' early Seventies 'floater' reflected Weller's increasing infatuation with black music. All three benefited from The Jam's newly-recruited brass section, and Paul's relaxed vocal style was particularly endearing.

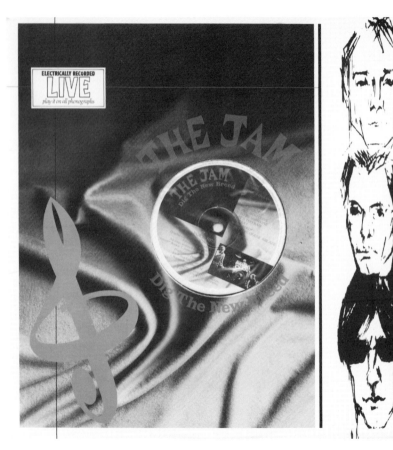

THE JAM LIVE

DIG THE NEW BREED

DATE: DECEMBER 1982
CHART POSITION: NO. 2
ORIGINAL LP: POLYDOR POLD 5075
CURRENT CD: POLYDOR 810 041-2

The Jam's recorded history didn't end on that emotional night on 11th December 1982. Taking its title from an old James Brown classic, *Dig The New Breed* was a live album issued that very month, not only as a fitting epitaph for a band whose tours were as important to their fans as their records, but also because (more specifically) The Jam still owed Polydor another album.

The disc was tastefully packaged in the style of an old black-and-white Sixties LP, the uncluttered white back cover leaving room for three very different farewells. Paul's was written in dramatic pop-art prose; Bruce's was serious and emotional; Rick's was honest and straightforward.

Dig The New Breed was a solid, representative overview of The Jam in concert, spanning their whole career. There was no sign of some promised pre-Polydor material from 1975, and with only one 1977 recording and two-thirds of the selections taped in the Eighties, the LP was weighted towards their more recent shows, reflecting Weller's low opinion of their pre-*All Mod Cons* work.

IN THE CITY

The 100 Club, London, 11/9/77

One of two Jam gigs across consecutive nights at Oxford Street's legendary basement was taped for possible release as a live album (which has since been bootlegged). Acetates were cut but the project was scrapped, aside from the live B-sides to 'The Modern World' single (see later) — and this album selection.

STANDARDS
Reading University, 16/2/79

ALL MOD CONS
TO BE SOMEONE
IT'S TOO BAD
The Rainbow, London, 13/12/79.

(This concert actually dated from 3rd December 1979.)

START!
BIG BIRD
SET THE HOUSE ABLAZE
Hammersmith Palais, London 14/12/81

The highlight of *Dig The New Breed* was a blistering cover of 'Big Bird'. This rock/soul/funk workout substituted the graceful power of Eddie Floyd's '68 Stax original for grit and aggression, creating a 'Trans-Global Express'-like anthem.

Alongside 'Move On Up', this was The Jam's most successful foray into soul.

GHOSTS
Bingley Hall, Birmingham, 21/3/82

IN THE CROWD
Edinburgh Playhouse, 6/4/82

GOING UNDERGROUND
THE DREAMS OF CHILDREN
THAT'S ENTERTAINMENT
PRIVATE HELL
Glasgow Apollo, 8/4/82

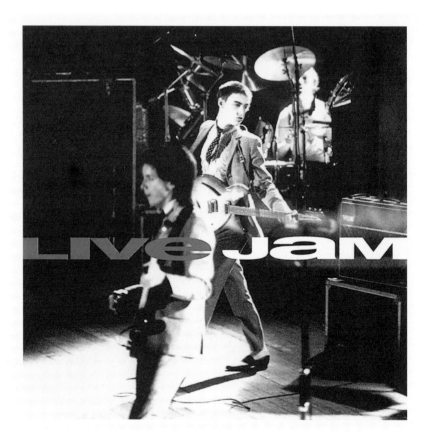

LIVE JAM

DATE: OCTOBER 1993

CHART POSITION: NO. 28

ORIGINAL 2-LP/CD: POLYDOR 519 667-1/2

This belated follow-up to *Dig The New Breed* stuck with the same formula, avoiding early material and sticking with just a handful of the numerous recorded Jam concerts . *Live Jam* had been tentatively titled 'Amplification' but Polydor got cold feet and changed their minds at the last moment. Although live recordings exist of The Jam covering soul classics like Chairmen Of The Board's 'Give Me Just A Little More Time' and the Four Tops' 'Reach Out, I'll Be There', plus The Who's 'Much Too Much' from 1977, none were deemed to be of sufficiently high quality for this release.

THE MODERN WORLD
BILLY HUNT
THICK AS THIEVES
BURNING SKY
MR. CLEAN
SMITHERS-JONES
LITTLE BOY SOLDIERS
AWAY FROM THE NUMBERS
DOWN IN THE TUBE
STATION AT MIDNIGHT

Rainbow, London, 2 & 3/12/79

'Away From The Numbers', 'The Modern World' and 'Down In The Tube Station At Midnight' were originally part of the double pack of 'Going Underground', before being recycled on several reissue singles.

STRANGE TOWN

Brighton Centre, 15/12/79

THE ETON RIFLES
WHEN YOU'RE YOUNG
'A' BOMB IN WARDOUR STREET

Newcastle City Hall, 26/10/80

PRETTY GREEN
BOY ABOUT TOWN
MAN IN THE CORNER SHOP
DAVID WATTS
FUNERAL PYRE
TOWN CALLED MALICE
Hammersmith Palais, 14 & 15/12/81

'Town Called Malice' had already graced the original 12" single.

HEATWAVE
Edinburgh Playhouse, 6/4/82

MOVE ON UP
CARNATION
Glasgow Apollo, 8/4/82

THE BUTTERFLY COLLECTOR
PRECIOUS
Wembley Arena, 2/12/82

NON-ALBUM
LIVE SONGS

SWEET SOUL MUSIC
BACK IN MY ARMS AGAIN
BRICKS AND MORTAR (Part)
100 Club, London, 11/9/77

The Jam threw themselves at break-neck speed through two Sixties soul classics, Arthur Conley's 'Sweet Soul Music' and The Supremes' 'Back In My Arms Again', chosen as the B-side to 'The Modern World' in October 1977. This was a fair reflection of The Jam's live set, which also featured, on occasion, Lee Dorsey's 'Ride Your Pony' (described by *Melody Maker*'s Brian Harrigan as "fast, crisp and raunchy") and Martha & the Vandellas' 'Heatwave', later recorded for the album *Setting Sons*.

MOVE ON UP
GET YOURSELF TOGETHER
THE GREAT DEPRESSION
BUT I'M DIFFERENT NOW
Wembley Arena, 2 & 3/12/82

An EP was given away with initial copies of the Jam retrospective album, *Snap!* (1983). 'Move On Up' was the Curtis Mayfield classic already recorded for the 'Beat Surrender' double pack. 'Get Yourself Together' was an old Small Faces song from their 1967 album, *Small Faces*, a studio demo of which was later unveiled on *Extras*. But these live recordings have never been transferred to CD.

MOVE ON UP

Another live version of 'Move On Up' (with an introduction suggesting it was taped in Japan) was given away on a flexidisc with *Melody Maker*. Again, this has never been reissued.

WHEN YOU'RE YOUNG

The first of two Jam fan club flexidiscs featured a live version of 'When You're Young'. This may have been the same recording which appeared on an *NME* cassette, *Dancin' Master*, in late 1981.

THE PEEL SESSIONS

DATE: SEPTEMBER 1990

ORIGINAL 12"/CD: STRANGE FRUIT SFPS/SFPSCD 080

CURRENT CD: STRANGE FRUIT SFPSCD 080 (DIFFERENT ARTWORK)

IN THE CITY/ART SCHOOL/I'VE CHANGED MY ADDRESS/MODERN WORLD

The Jam recorded the first of three sessions for John Peel's Radio One show on 26th April 1977, on the eve of the release of their first album. The first three songs were taken from the album (and didn't differ greatly). But the fourth song pre-empted its choice as a single by some six months. Neither of The Jam's subsequent Peel sessions, nor their subsequent session with Kid Jensen, has been officially released.

THE JAM EXTRAS

THE JAM:
COMPILATION ALBUMS

EXTRAS

DATE: APRIL 1992
CHART POSITION: NO. 15
ORIGINAL 2-LP/CD: POLYDOR 513 177-1/2

Extras was a remarkable collection because roughly half the material was previously unissued. Many of the songs were Paul Weller's solo demos of familiar Jam songs: 'Liza Radley', 'Burning Sky', 'Thick As Thieves', 'But I'm Different Now', 'Saturday's Kids', and 'The Eton Rifles'. Others were newly uncovered versions of old Sixties tunes: The Beatles' 'And Your Bird Can Sing', the Small Faces' 'Get Yourself Together' and James Brown's 'I Got You (I Feel Good)'. Most exciting were a handful of 'new' songs: 'No One In The World', 'Hey Mister' and 'We've Only Started', plus a Jam version of the later Style Council single, 'A Solid Bond In Your Heart'.

BURNING SKY
THICK AS THIEVES
SATURDAY'S KIDS
THE ETON RIFLES

Weller's solo demos for *Setting Sons* were mostly (if not all) taped at Polydor's Stratford Place Studios in June/July 1979, prior to the album sessions at Town House. Not only do these illustrate which songs Paul took to the sessions (as opposed to those written in situ in the studio), but also that, despite their primitive nature, each was pretty well complete, both structurally and lyrically.

HEY MISTER

Some confusion still surrounds this *Extras* discovery. The sleeve-notes claim it dated from 1979, although Weller has suggested the song was written during sessions for *Sound Affects*. Whatever its source, 'Hey Mister' was a straightforward jibe at politicians but is notable as one of the rare occasions Paul sang accompanied only by piano.

LIZA RADLEY
AND YOUR BIRD CAN SING
BUT I'M DIFFERENT NOW

Weller's rediscovery of The Beatles' *Revolver* album in 1979/1980 seems to have had nearly as a profound effect on him as hearing The Who's *My Generation* back in the mid-Seventies. Hence this faithful if pedestrian run through John Lennon's 'And Your Bird Can Sing', taped at Polydor in April 1980, prior to sessions for *Sound Affects*. The song was never planned for release but this demo sounds respectably professional, later described by Weller as "just a bit of fun, me with

Pete Wilson playing drums. From that, you get other ideas." 'But I'm Different Now' was taped during the same sessions, a dry run for *Sound Affects*; 'Liza Radley' was reworked for the B-side to 'Start!'.

NO ONE IN THE WORLD

Recorded at Polydor's Stratford Place studios in September 1980, this plaintive, introspective ballad relied on a similar guitar riff as 'Mr. Clean' from *All Mod Cons*, and a break which was eventually used for 'Monday' on *Sound Affects*.

"It was never used because it didn't go anywhere," confessed Weller. "It only had those two changes and I couldn't finish it. There's a major-to-minor chord change I used on a lot of Jam records, especially around that time."

GET YOURSELF TOGETHER

Weller's admiration for Sixties band the Small Faces is well-documented, a lifelong love first documented on vinyl in 1983, when a live version of 'Get Yourself Together' appeared on a freebie single with the *Snap!* Retrospective. A decade later, *Extras* revealed that a studio demo existed, too, dating from July 1981. It's possibly the strongest cover The Jam ever performed, and their characteristic bite retaining the energetic passion of the original, although Weller's re-vocal (re-recorded especially for *Extras*) couldn't hope to match Steve Marriott's uniquely soulful tones. The song had been a highlight of the 1967 album, *Small Faces*.

I GOT YOU (I FEEL GOOD)

The Jam playing James Brown? Well, the experiment did't pay off, so talk of a covers EP, leading off with this 1966 classic, had quietly been dropped. Again, Paul was an ardent fan of the 'Godfather Of Soul' (remember that line from 'Non-Stop Dancing'?), and The Jam's rendition was surprisingly tight, but lacked the vital spark of the original. "My voice is a bit strange," Paul later admitted. "My vocals are fucking awful, actually, so I wasn't happy with it!"

WE'VE ONLY STARTED

If 'Solid Bond In Your Heart' was the closest thing to an unissued Jam single, this ran a close second. Taped in August 1981, 'We've Only Started' swiftly evolved into 'Tales From The Riverbank' (which was completed the following month). This demo is far more frenetic, with a different lyrics and a heavier feel, partly because it was recorded a year or so earlier when The Jam's sound was more punky.

A SOLID BOND IN YOUR HEART

This Northern Soul-inspired track was finally issued as a Style Council single in late 1983. Exactly a year earlier, the song was mooted as a possibility as The Jam's final single – but 'Beat Surrender' was chosen instead. Aside from The Jam's vibe-dominated intro (perhaps borrowed from Judy Street's Northern Soul classic, 'What', as covered by Soft Cell), the versions are quite similar. A second Jam version, which shared the same middle eight as 'Beat Surrender', later surfaced on the Jam box set.

DIRECTION REACTION CREATION:
THE JAM BOX SET

DATE: MAY 1997

CHART POSITION: NO. 8

ORIGINAL 5-CD SET: POLYDOR 537 143-2

Direction, Reaction, Creation was one of the fastest-selling box sets ever issued in Britain – and certainly the highest-charting. Unlike most such collections, which attempt to straddle two stools – rarities and classics – this five-CD set combined The Jam's entire recorded output with a whole CD of demos.

Well, that's not strictly true. Only the later version of 'War' was included. There wasn't room for the unissued material from *Extras*, nor the alternate mixes of 'Funeral Pyre' and 'That's Entertainment' from *Snap!* And The Jam's singles were often reworked for their albums – for example, 'Start!', 'The Eton Rifles', 'David Watts', ' 'A' Bomb' and 'Tube Station'. In most instances, only the album versions were chosen for the box set. The exceptions were 'Precious' (the elongated 12" version was used) and 'Start!' (the 7" mix was chosen). But *Direction, Reaction, Creation* was still effectively the definitive collection of The Jam.

What follows is a breakdown of that fifth CD of new material.

IN THE CITY
TIME FOR TRUTH
SOUNDS FROM
THE STREET
SO SAD ABOUT US
(February 1977)

Polydor invited The Jam into the studio for a demo session before signing them. This was the result: three songs which would later appear on their first album, plus a cover of The Who's 'So Sad About Us', re-recorded around September 1978 as the B-side to 'Down In The Tube Station At Midnight'.

WORLDS APART
(February 1978)

Although rumours of an abandoned third album were more fiction than fact, Jam researcher Dennis Munday unearthed this charming demo from early 1978. Presumably taped in the wake of sessions for 'News Of The World' but before the band's infamous trip to America that spring, 'Worlds Apart' was a jolly, carefree Weller song, based

around the piano rather than the guitar – unusual for someone still embroiled in a more aggressive new wave sound. (Another Jam song from this period, 'She's Got Everything', dated from the 'News Of The World' sessions. Although it was cut to acetate, no master tape exists in Polydor's vaults and so the track evaded the box set.)

BILLY HUNT
IT'S TOO BAD
TO BE SOMEONE
DAVID WATTS
(June 1978)

Demos for *All Mod Cons*, cut in June 1978. This rougher version of 'Billy Hunt' had been planned as a single, to be backed by 'English Rose' and 'The Night', but The Jam had a change of heart and issued 'David Watts' instead.

BEST OF BOTH WORLDS
(September 1979)

Recorded during the tail-end of sessions for *Setting Sons* in 1979, this Bruce Foxton song wasn't deemed strong enough for the final LP. Nearly two decades on, the song's appearance validates that decision.

THAT'S ENTERTAINMENT
RAIN
DREAM TIME
DEAD END STREET
(April/September 1980)

The alternative version of 'That's Entertainment' which appeared on *Snap!* back in 1983 featured only Weller; both Bruce and Rick were heard on this third variant. More exciting was 'Rain', a cover of The Beatles' B-side to 'Paperback Writer' (recorded around the same time as 'And Your Bird Can Sing'), Weller joined by Pete Wilson (drums and Hammond organ) and roadie Dave Liddle (guitar). Both these demos were taped at Polydor's studios in early April 1980, prior to the start of the *Sound Affects* sessions later that month at Town House.

'Dream Time' was radically different from its eventual incarnation – an unusual scenario because Weller normally presented demos as finished songs. In contrast to the swirling intensity of the finished article, this rough prototype is totally acoustic, with shaky vocal overdubs, recorded during the first few days' work on *Sound Affects*. An affectionate run through The Kinks' 'Dead End Street' dated from September that year – with Pete Wilson as his only accomplice.

STAND BY ME
EVERY LITTLE BIT HURTS

More evidence of Weller's love affair with Sixties soul. His (undated) attempt at Ben E. King's 'Stand By Me' was probably best left alone. Brenda Holloway's 'Every Little Bit Hurts', on the other hand, was treated with the care and attention it deserved. This mid-Sixties Motown classic was covered during sessions for 'Absolute Beginners' at AIR London Studios in August 1981.

TALES FROM THE RIVERBANK

The B-side to 'Absolute Beginners' was re-recorded a couple of months later in November 1981 with The Jam's new twin-piece horn section. Weller always regretted relegating the song to a flip-side and considered this new version for *The Gift*. Instead, it was sent out as a fan club flexidisc in February 1982. Some of the song's atmospheric intro-spection was lost in the process but the two versions illustrate how The Jam were changing from a dense, vaguely psychedelic approach to a more upbeat sound rooted in old – and new – soul.

WALKING IN HEAVEN'S SUNSHINE

One of the real gems of *Direction, Reaction, Creation* was this breezy effort which, although undated, proba-bly stemmed from the same sessions in mid-1982 which yielded 'Pity Poor Alfie'. Certainly, their feel was very simi-lar, from the strident Cockney-ish piano

(which punctuates 'Walking In Heaven's Sunshine' with little fills) to Weller's vocal (which threatens to break into a falsetto). The rhythm of the middle eight was later heard in the Style Council song, 'Headstart For Happiness'.

PRECIOUS

The absence of demos for *The Gift* on both *Extras* and the box set was surprising – and 'Precious' was merely a rough working copy of the finished product, dating from the first batch of sessions in November 1981.

PITY POOR ALFIE

This 'swing' version of the eventual B-side to 'The Bitterest Pill' was taped at AIR Studios in early February 1982, probably in down time at the very end of mixing for *The Gift*. The music shuffles in with the atmosphere of dimmed lighting, the funky bass joined by stabs of organ, sax and light percussion. Weller's voice sounds relaxed – though it's patently just a guide vocal. What's more remarkable is the backing music, which sounds far more fluid and funky than anything else by The Jam. In fact, this alone could represent a prototype for The Style Council, what with the jazzy Hammond organ runs (courtesy of Steve Nichol) and a groove that wouldn't have seemed out of place on the late Eighties Acid Jazz scene. Was that really Bruce and Rick?

THE BITTEREST PILL (I EVER HAD TO SWALLOW)

Recorded at London's Odyssey Studios (probably in early summer '82), this prototype for The Jam's second-to-last single added an awkward, cod-Sixties break towards the end. Otherwise, this finished dry run actually sounded more comfortable than its more familiar cousin, from Weller's voice to the string arrangements and the overall production.

A SOLID BOND IN YOUR HEART

Unsure as to the final Jam single, Weller juggled with both 'Beat Surrender' and this eventual Style Council single. The major difference between this and the version which had earlier graced *Extras* was the middle eight, which was essentially the same as that which appeared in 'Beat Surrender'.

OTHER COMPILATION ALBUMS

SNAP!

DATE: OCTOBER 1983
CHART POSITION: NO. 2
ORIGINAL 2-LP: POLYDOR SNAP 1 513 177-1
CURRENT CD: POLYDOR 815 537-2

Polydor's official retrospective paid handsome tribute to The Jam, from the sensible track listing (mixing classic hits with album highlights and the odd B-side) to the stylish packaging, which included a free live EP taped at Wembley during the band's final tour. 'Funeral Pyre' was remixed because Weller wasn't happy with the original single while his own solo demo of 'That's Entertainment' spoke volumes about his opinion of the ballad in the hands of Bruce and Rick.

GREATEST HITS

DATE: JUNE 1991
CHART POSITION: NO. 2
ORIGINAL LP/CD: POLYDOR 849 554-1/2
CURRENT CD: POLYDOR 849 554-2

Weller had scarcely launched his solo career before Polydor whittled down *Snap!* into this more marketable collection of the band's singles. The packaging was terrible but sales were healthy, prompting a wave of subsequent retrospectives from Polydor of both The Jam and The Style Council.

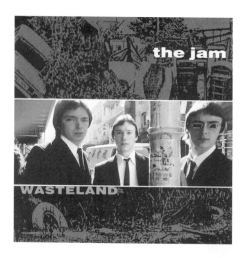

WASTELAND

DATE: OCTOBER 1992

ORIGINAL CD: PICKWICK PWKS 4129P

Having The Jam on Pickwick felt like issuing a Beatles compilation on K-Tel. However, this budget collection of their earlier recordings at least helped keep The Jam's music accessible to a younger audience.

BEAT SURRENDER

DATE: MAY 1993

ORIGINAL CD: SPECTRUM 550 006-2

At the time, this pointless, arbitrarily-compiled mid-price collection was the only way of hearing 'Carnaby Street' on CD. Write to Polydor requesting its deletion today!

THE JAM COLLECTION

DATE: JULY 1996

CHART POSITION: NO. 58

ORIGINAL 2-LP/CD: POLYDOR 531 493-1/2

The Jam might have been dismissed as a singles band by those who hadn't heard their LPs. In which case, *The Jam Collection* would have been the doubter's first port of call, since it assembled an intelligent cross-section of the band's more thoughtful, melodic songs.

Introducing *The Style Council*

THE STYLE COUNCIL: STUDIO ALBUMS

INTRODUCING THE STYLE COUNCIL

DATE: SEPTEMBER 1983

ORIGINAL MINI-LP: DUTCH IMPORT, POLYDOR 815 277-1

CURRENT CD: POLYDOR 815 277-2

From the outset, The Style Council appeared to be at polar opposites to The Jam. Whereas The Jam were perceived as an earnest, guitar-driven 'rock' band with a loyal live following, The Style Council were presented as a laid-back, non-rock collective who shunned the album-tour-album rigmarole for a floating line-up, a string of non-album singles and no touring. If The Jam were proper, then The Style Council, with their impish sense of humour, were improper.

But Weller's transition from punk vitriol into soul boy smoothness was far less linear (or sudden) than the history books would have us believe. Lyrically, The Style Council could be far more aggressive than The Jam – and more focussed, in terms of individual causes. And The Jam's last album, *The Gift* (and subsequent singles), softened the blow, introducing a more soulful make-up that bridged the gap between The Jam's post-punk angularity and The Style Council's slicker approach.

In effect, The Jam had always been the Paul Weller Roadshow. It's just that, in Weller's view, there was a train-a-comin' (to paraphrase Curtis Mayfield) and Bruce and Rick were unable to get on board. So the only real difference between The Jam's swansong, 'Beat Surrender' and The Style Council's debut, 'Speak Like A Child', was the rhythm section.

'Speak Like A Child' kickstarted a

string of diverse singles, all of them hits despite a lack of UK dates or an album: the minimal, uncompromising rap of 'Money-Go-Round', the bitter-sweet soul ballad, 'Long Hot Summer', and the Northern Soul-fuelled 'Solid Bond In Your Heart'; each very different and yet collectively reflecting Weller's shedding of The Jam straitjacket.

To plug the gap before their début album proper, a Dutch mini-album, *Introducing The Style Council*, was imported en masse, though we've chosen to document the songs as they appeared on 45, as a more accurate reflection of how they were heard at the time.

The track listing for *Introducing...* was as follows:
'Long Hot Summer (Extended Version)' /'Headstart For Happiness' / 'Speak Like A Child' / 'Long Hot Summer (Club Mix)' / 'The Paris Match' / 'Mick's Up' / 'Money-Go-Round'

SPEAK LIKE A CHILD

Orange Juice's drummer, the Zimbabwean-born Zeke Manyika, played on The Style Council's début. Issued in early March 1983, the single ushered in a new age for Weller – maybe it was a coincidence but the 7"-only package in a plain black sleeve (coloured only by the band's name and a Northern Soul-like 'keeps on burning' logo) echoed the design for The Sex Pistols' début, 'Anarchy In The UK', so treasured by Paul back in late 1976. No-one claimed that 'Speak Like A Child' was as revolutionary a statement as 'Anarchy' but, for Weller at least, it was the manifestation of a bold musical rethink. The record sold over 350,000 copies without even a picture of the group on the front.

It was also a wonderful pop record. The song had a faint Motown feel but its sound was fresh and modern – with Paul's funky bass line, Mick's smooth, high-pitched keyboards, the shrill brass and the synth-drum crashes. And

Tracie's backing vocals were closer to a duet with Paul in places.

PARTY CHAMBERS

The B-side, 'Party Chambers', was driven by piano, topped with Mick's now-dated, squeaky synth. The single also introduced the Cappuccino Kid, a fictional sleeve-note writer that came to symbolise both The Style Council's most self-indulgent excesses and Weller's very real attempt to inject humour into the band. This "geezer we bump into around the cafés and restaurants of the West End" was in fact journalist Paolo Hewitt, with a little help from Paul: expressed in ornate, mock-19th-century prose, the Cappuccino Kid's thoughts were sometimes amusing, sometimes impenetrable, always pretentious.

Later that year, 'Party Chambers' was reworked as a jazzy instrumental on the *A Paris EP*, giving Talbot free rein to mix Hammond organ and piano.

MONEY-GO-ROUND

Issued on May 20 1983, 'Money-Go-Round' was a tense if slightly stilted funk jam, named after an old Kinks song, which suited Weller's lyrical rap about the evils of capitalism and imperialism. The lyrics attacked the financial and military status quo, questioning why there hadn't been a referendum on U.S. bases and Cruise – the logical extension of Weller's involvement with CND, dating back to 1981.

To follow 'Speak Like A Child' with such an overtly political theme was a bold one. After all, radio exposure was bound to be minimal. But Weller has rarely played the pop game and he had a statement to make – though its Britfunk groove had a tough commercial edge reminiscent of Spandau Ballet's 'Chant No. 1'. As it transpired, 'Money-Go-Round' reached a respectable No. 11 in the UK, and the author's considerable royalties were donated to Youth CND.

The backing track dated from their earliest sessions, alongside 'Headstart For

Happiness' and 'A Solid Bond In Your Heart', born out of an impromptu jam with Wham! backing singer Dee C. Lee and I Level bassist Jo Dworniak – which is why it had no proper start, hence an introduction from jazz trombonist Annie Whitehead. The song's lyrics were then added afterwards.

The song was also Weller's first to be given a remix, a technique still unusual at the time for records other than those aimed at the clubs; Bert Bevan's mix was available on a European 12" and the mini-album, and now appears on the box set, *The Complete Adventures Of The Style Council*.

HEADSTART FOR HAPPINESS

On the B-side, the tuneful 'Headstart For Happiness' was a summery acoustic song that remains one of Weller's most endearing compositions, a reflection of a new spirit of optimism which ran through his lyrics, in stark contrast to the grittiness of 'Money-Go-Round'. The song was reworked on their debut LP, *Café Bleu*.

MICK'S UP

The third track on 'Money-Go-Round', Talbot's 'Mick's Up', was the first in a series of groovy, Jimmy Smith-inspired Hammond organ instrumentals. These paved the way for late-Eighties acts like the James Taylor Quartet and Corduroy, who seemed to base their entire career around the same sound.

LONG HOT SUMMER

In June 1983, The Style Council visited Paris, a trip which resulted in a new single, as well as reels of photos of Weller and Talbot posing in brightly-coloured woollens in front of various Parisian landmarks. The imagery perfectly matched the atmosphere of the resulting *A Paris EP*, issued in August – four tunes which, according to the cover, "all had a similar 'Blue Mood' and a certain French flavour about them". Indeed, the liner notes to the 7" were completely in French, as were the adverts in the press.

The lead song, 'Long Hot Summer', was the type of love-laden ballad which Weller had earlier explored with 'The Bitterest Pill', though the yearning nakedness of The Jam's earlier serenades ('English Rose', for example) was absent. Still, the feel suited its title perfectly, capturing the mood while the sun was shining. The video followed suit, Weller bearing his chest as he and Mick punted down a Cambridge river. New drummer Steve White added some bongos but the track's smooth, modern production and the "shoo-be doo-be, doo-be doo-wap" refrain brought to mind the kind of bland soul stylings of Imagination. Having criticised other chart groups, Weller had now created the ultimate in mainstream pop. But for every 'Long Hot Summer', there was a 'Money-Go-Round'.

'Long Hot Summer' was revisited on several occasions during The Style Council's lifespan: on 1988's *1-2-3-4* EP and as a newly remixed single to promote 1989's *Singular Adventures...* collection.

THE PARIS MATCH

The strongest moment on *A Paris* was *The Paris Match*, named after the city's principal magazine. Poignantly accompanied by accordion, some sensitive guitar playing and Mick's piano, this mournful, beautiful ballad ranks among Weller's finest-ever compositions. The lyrics were punning and clever, creating a sensitive, imaginative romantic ode far more sophisticated than, say, 'Long Hot Summer'. Again, the song was re-worked for *Café Bleu*.

LE DÉPART

'Le Départ' was a ponderous, atmospheric piano instrumental by Talbot (the EP sleeve humorously claimed that the piece was to be used as the theme for a new French film called *The Golden Lama* starring one Alain Mélon).

A SOLID BOND IN YOUR HEART

Taped at the start of the year, 'A Solid Bond In Your Heart' was finally issued in November 1983, having not only been considered for The Jam's swansong a year earlier (two Jam prototypes have belatedly surfaced on retrospectives) but also as the TSC debut. The song's uplifting, shout-it-from-the-rooftops message suited its Northern Soul feel – the synth strings, the "on-the-fours" beat from Zeke Manyika (his last contribution to the Council), and some driving saxophone from Chris Hunter.

IT JUST CAME TO PIECES IN MY HANDS

The other side of the single, 'It Just Came To Pieces In My Hands', was an edgy, primitively-recorded solo guitar ballad, decorated only by some doo wop-styled backing vocals. Paul described the song's message as representing "blind foolishness of conceit".

CAFÉ BLEU · THE STYLE COUNCIL

CAFÉ BLEU

DATE: MARCH 1984
CHART POSITION: NO. 2
ORIGINAL LP: POLYDOR TSCLP 1
CURRENT CD: POLYDOR 817 535-2

Judging by early reports, The Style Council's début album would be ambitious. "It's a double LP – one side romantic, slightly sad, a bit moody," said Paul. "The second side more funky; the third with today's pop songs; and the fourth remixes of the singles."

Café Bleu, followed in March. For all its strengths, the album sounds positively schizophrenic today. From rap to jazz, soul to acoustic ballads, Hammond organ instrumentals to guitar pop, love songs to political diatribes, it offered a potpourri of sounds and textures. Eclectic and ambitious, *Café Bleu* was very much in keeping with the mid-Eighties' music scene's anti-rock stance. And, if Mods were magpies, then Weller had rummaged through the nooks and crannies of music past and present.

Like the 12" edition of 'My Ever Changing Moods', and in keeping with the album's title, *Café Bleu*'s tastefully designed sleeve carried a blue-tinted photo of Mick and Paul outside a Parisian café – as did the novel A5 lyric booklet inside, prefaced by an affected four-page story from the Cappuccino Kid. The French connection was taken a step further by a quote on the rear sleeve from '18th-Century French visionary', Jean Paul Marat. This propagandist and heroic martyr for the extreme left-wing died in the French Revolution, having prophesied the invention of weapons which would, "with a flick of the finger, tear a million of you to pieces". This patently reflected Paul's continued commitment to CND.

The whole package was the product of intense attention to detail, and a victory for Paul, whose complete conviction led to power struggles with Polydor and (what Weller viewed as) their unimaginative, 'hard sell' policies. The double-album idea of four distinct themes across each side hadn't materialised. Instead, they were squashed into two: the first half of *Café Bleu* introduced the jazzier, more atmospheric music; the second was brasher, more upbeat and less moody. It felt like the difference between winter and summer.

Instead of filling up the album with old singles, three of the band's strongest tunes were re-recorded: 'Headstart For Happiness', 'My Ever Changing Moods' and 'The Paris Match'. Of the thirteen tracks, five were instrumentals and Paul sang only six of the remainder. This endorsed his earlier statements about avoiding a central player – although it was clear Weller was in charge. The instrumentals were an adventurous ploy on Weller's part, adding light and shade rather than suggesting he had run short of songs, dabbling in different styles of jazz (some brazenly lifted from old classics) and rhythm'n'soul.

The range of musicians on the LP was as broad as the music itself. Chris Bostock, from Northern Soul-styled pop band Jo Boxers, played double bass on 'Here's One That Got Away'; Animal Nightlife saxophonist Billy Chapman helped out on some of the jazz tracks; and other guests included rapper Dizzy Hites, old friends Everything But The Girl and session musicians like trumpeter Barbara Snow and saxophonist Hillary Seabrook. Drummer Steve White was the most significant addition to the fold. In fact, the band's nucleus had effectively grown into a trio – White was pictured on the back sleeve, alongside Weller and Talbot.

Café Bleu received a mixed reaction – the album was slated by rock-heavy music weekly *Sounds* as "dispensable dross" -- but it only narrowly missed out on the No. 1 spot and spent eight months in the charts, a longer period than that of any of The Jam's albums. The Style Council were proving themselves to be one of the most vital and creative forces within the British pop scene of the mid-Eighties.

MICK'S BLESSINGS

Talbot's third and last of his "Mick's" instrumentals opened *Café Bleu* in buoyant mood, a jaunty piano piece with a boogie woogie tilt and a solid Sixties soul rhythm.

THE WHOLE POINT OF NO RETURN

Only twelve titles were listed on the *Café Bleu* sleeve: this song was added at the very last moment and the covers had already been printed by the time Paul had recorded the song. This eloquent attack on Britain's class system was set to a beautiful tune, accompanied only by some jazzy guitar. Weller has rarely bettered the song's intensity and atmosphere, his heartfelt anger at the injustices of inherited wealth made all the more poignant by its musical subtlety. He'd come a long way from his days of brash punk polemic.

ME SHIP CAME IN!

The perky Latin fusion feel of 'Me Ship Came In!' was further proof of Weller's jazz indulgences; the Blue Note influence patently reached further than the artwork and Weller later confessed that he had borrowed the refrain from Horace Silver's classic title track, 'Song For My Father'.

BLUE CAFÉ

This smoky jazz guitar instrumental was the most sublime moment on the album, provoking images of a hazy basement club in Soho, circa '59. Steve White's jazz training blossomed via his deft use of the brushes and Weller's guitar playing sounded effortless.

THE PARIS MATCH

This highlight from the *A Paris EP* was given over to Ben Watt and Tracey Thorn from Everything But The Girl, who lent the song a bluesy torch singer vibe. Watt's chordal jazz guitar playing fascinated Weller, apparently. Indeed, the pair had lent Paul tapes of their forth-coming debut LP, *Eden*, which must have influenced his approach to *Café Bleu*. A third recording of the song exists by Dee C. Lee, backed by 'the Council Quartet' on her 1985 hit, 'See The Day'.

MY EVER CHANGING MOODS

In February '84, a couple of months prior to the album, The Style Council issued one of Weller's strongest songs and most eloquent lyrics, the sprightly 'My Ever Changing Moods'. The title implied some admission of his own temperament, but the mood swing in question had as much to do with Paul's observations of the changes in public attitudes and social policy under Thatcherism as his own personality. It was about "how the important issues in life are obscured by trivialities," he observed at the time.

With 'My Ever Changing Moods', Weller also created what might be described as The Style Council's sound.

In 1983, Paul had dabbled and experi-mented with different ideas, finding his feet and exploring new possibilities. But their fifth single was more cohesive; Weller discovered a less abrasive guitar tone he was happy with, and returned to the instrument for a heart-lifting solo, while the tune itself had that yearning, personal quality which characterises his best songs.

It still felt modern, though: producer Pete Wilson played bass synth and Paul's soulful vocal style meant it was easy to imagine contemporary artists like Culture Club's Boy George or George Michael singing the melody. Despite its lyrical edge, this was 100% pop music, horns and all. Not only did the band notch up another massive domestic hit, but Weller enjoyed his first taste of the Stateside success when it made the Top 40 there.

The album version was completely re-recorded, with each verse tackled by different band members – Paul, Mick and Dee. The pace was slowed some-what, and the lyrics were more audible.

DROPPING BOMBS ON THE WHITEHOUSE

The clear-cut, straight-ahead bop of 'Dropping Bombs On The Whitehouse' was arguably the most successful jazz excursion on *Café Bleu*. In concert, the song was sometimes segued into a cover of Funkadelic's 'One Nation Under A Groove'.

A GOSPEL

Weller's second of four rap explorations with The Style Council (the others being 'Money-Go-Round', 'Soul Deep' and 'Right To Go') has dated more rapidly than the rest of *Café Bleu*. But its revolutionary theme was delivered with style by Dizzy Hites, a London-based singer whose previous claim to fame was his minor novelty hit with 1982's 'Christmas Rapping'. Dizzy later recorded his own version of Weller's poetic rant at Solid Bond Studios, aided by Steve White on drums and issued as 'The Gospel!' on EMI in early 1985.

STRENGTH OF YOUR NATURE

Dee C. Lee sang on this neo-funk anthem, which echoed Heaven 17's skill at mixing dancefloor rhythms with the latest technical developments in synths and drum programmers ('Fascist Groove Thang', for example). The repetitive melody of 'Strength Of Your Nature' was seemingly borrowed from Lee Dorsey's soul classic, 'Working In A Coalmine'; its chant-like structure seemed to pick up where The Jam's "Trans-Global Express" left off.

YOU'RE THE BEST THING

Issued in the wake of the album as a single (in remixed form), 'You're The Best Thing' was firmly rooted in the 'Long Hot Summer' mould; only the backing music was more intricate, from Paul's delicate guitar to Billy Chapman's saxophone. With its Impressions-like falsetto chorus, this lush, soulful ballad constituted Weller's most blatant stab at a straightforward pop song so far –

and it worked beautifully. The catchy tune gave the band another Top 5 hit and seemed to be on permanent rotation on the radio throughout summer 1984.

HERE'S ONE THAT GOT AWAY

The gentle, summer pop swing of 'Here's One That Got Away' was one of the album's most uplifting moments. Weller was evidently the escapee in question. Though the subject of his wrath ("I felt so sick I spat on their lifestyles") wasn't transparent, the critics were probably the target (with that line, "They tried to tell me I wasn't full time").

HEADSTART FOR HAPPINESS

Paul, Mick and Dee C. Lee shared verses on a fuller-sounding rendition of 'Headstart For Happiness', which remains one of the most popular Style Council songs to this day. Its position after 'Here's One That Got Away' was a

majestic stroke, maintaining an upbeat atmosphere to offset the more contemplative atmosphere of the first half of the LP.

COUNCIL MEETIN'

Café Bleu ended in an upbeat party groove with the dancefloor-friendly 'Council Meetin' ', a swinging Northern Soul-meets-Hammond organ affair with heavy (black) shades of a Sixties Ramsey Lewis.

NON-ALBUM SONGS

MICK'S COMPANY

As a single, 'My Ever Changing Moods' was joined by two other tracks, beginning with another of Talbot's organ workouts, 'Mick's Company'.

SPRING, SUMMER, AUTUMN

The second B-side was this delicate acoustic ode, 'Spring, Summer, Autumn', a Weller composition disguised by the tongue-in-cheek pseudonym of

Jake Fluckery, a play on the name of folk singer Jake Thackray. A cover of Chairmen Of The Board's 'Hanging On To A Memory' had been planned as the B-side and artwork was even prepared, depicting a young child with a guitar (which might possibly have been Paul) and the slogan, "features excerpts from two hips from Amsterdam". The idea was shelved, though live versions of both songs belatedly surfaced on *In Concert*.

THE BIG BOSS GROOVE

'You're The Best Thing' was part of the double-A-sided *Groovin' EP*, but the song's success inadvertently dwarfed its companion, 'Big Boss Groove'. This modern R&B tune strutted along, driven by Mick's strident piano playing, a horn section and a finger-clicking soul back-beat – and a harmonica solo from Paul. The song's lyrics reiterated Weller's rallying cry that "together we can be so strong", as the supposed method of overthrowing those in power.

SHOUT TO THE TOP!

The Council's next single (autumn 1984) was supported by confrontational adverts that proclaimed: "Make no mistake /This is all class war/Fight back/Shout To The Top!". Those who expected a Marxist lecture were instead treated to arguably the band's most comfortable venture at combining their own sound with an authentic soul backbeat. Quite apart from the song's energetic vibe, 'Shout To The Top' worked because Mick's driving piano riff did all the legwork (like a faster 'Big Boss Groove') and the basic melody was mapped out using the strident, Philly-styled string arrangements of noted BBC theme composer John Mealing and Philadelphia veteran Jay Mark. Simple but effective, it gave the Council another sizeable hit. Despite his subsequent doubts, Weller's first stab at producing his own record was an unmitigated success.

Weller still believed that socialism was a viable proposition to present to the electorate. This message was evident on the sleeve: "No! To abolition of the GLC and the local councils. Yes! To a nuclear free world. Yes! To all involved in animal rights. Yes! To fanzines. Yes! To Belief." This was the first evidence of Paul's new-found support of animal rights activities. His girlfriend, Gill Price, had not only converted him to vegetarianism but opened his eyes to contentious issues like blood sports and animal testing.

'Shout To The Top' was belatedly added to the CD of the band's next album, *Our Favourite Shop*.

GHOSTS OF DACHAU

Both the single's B-sides were less upbeat. 'Ghosts Of Dachau' was an anguished ballad, based around the theme of the Nazi wartime concentration camp, with Weller's vocal straining and uncomfortable. "I really feel this is one of the best songs I've ever written," he commented. "I went to Dachau in 1978, it's just outside Munich in Germany, and still the place haunts you."

THE PICCADILLY TRAIL

Nearly as haunting was 'The Piccadilly Trail', which conjured up images of loneliness, especially with its contemplative lyrics like "I'm so scared of the weeks ahead". Its lovelorn theme seemed rooted in bitterness, culminating in the repetition of the word "betrayal", though the beguiling music disguised such feelings.

SOUL DEEP

By November 1984, Britain's ten-month-old miners' strike had weakened and men were gradually returning to work. But one of their unlikeliest allies, from their standpoint at least, was pop music. Weller hadn't been alone in actively endorsing socialist views; acts like Billy Bragg, The Mekons and The Redskins played benefit concerts and campaigned. But Paul took matters a stage further, hastily assembling a group of musicians to record a profile-raising single, 'Soul Deep', with money to be donated to an organisation known as Women Against Pit Closures.

The project was credited to The Council Collective – effectively The Style Council with a little help from friends Dee C. Lee, Dizzy Hites, Vaughn Toulouse and Animal Nightlife's Leonardo Chignoli, plus veteran U.S. Motown star Jimmy Ruffin (whose father was a miner) and British soul singer Junior Giscombe.

'Soul Deep' was a clumsy electro-funk track which sounded hurried – which wasn't surprising, since the backing track had been laid down in one day, and the vocals the next – but it reached its goal of publicising the miners' cause. However, the idea was very nearly shelved. On November 30, on the brink of the single's release, two miners were charged with murder after David Wilkie, a taxi driver in South Wales, who was ferrying strike-breakers to work, was killed by a concrete block which had been dropped onto his car from an overhead bridge.

A press release was circulated on December 5 regretting the cancellation of 'Soul Deep' for "artistic reasons".

This was probably a smoke-screen for Weller's indecision. Eventually, the single was issued and the sleeve-notes were changed: "The aim of this record was to raise money for the Striking Miners and their families before Xmas but obviously in the light of the tragic and disgusting event in South Wales, some of the monies will also go now to the widow of the man."

Despite the predictable lack of airplay (some radio stations and shops boycotted the single, as did some club DJs), 'Soul Deep' made the Top 30 and sold a healthy 100,000 copies. The result was a donation of nearly £10,000, helped by an anonymous-looking 12" remix.

A MINERS' POINT

Buried away on the B-side was an interview by journalist Paolo Hewitt with some of Nottingham's striking miners, which covered many of the critical issues – an intelligent device to communicate the salient arguments to purchasers ignorant of political issues.

THE STYLE COUNCIL/OUR FAVOURITE SHOP

OUR FAVOURITE SHOP

DATE: JUNE 1985

CHART POSITION: NO. 1

ORIGINAL LP: POLYDOR TSCLP 2

CURRENT CD: POLYDOR 825 700-2

Recording sessions for The Style Council's second LP commenced in February 1985, the International Year Of Youth, of which Weller was President. His first task was to attend a Youth Trade Union Rights Committee demonstration against the Government's attempt to create "industrial conscription". Within this climate, it was no surprise that their next single was confrontational – and sure enough, the rousing 'Walls Come Tumbling Down' had a snarl and a bite that Weller hadn't demonstrated since the Jam days.

On June 8, 1985, The Style Council's second album went to No. 1 – a crowning achievement for Paul Weller. To him, *Our Favourite Shop* felt like the best LP he had ever made. "This record is so important to me," he wrote. "I've spent so much time over the lyrics. It's also more organ and guitar-based. I've never believed so positively in any record."

The eye-catching gatefold sleeve design was the visual embodiment of the album's title, picturing Paul and Mick immersed in a 'room' chock-a-block with clothes, books, records, photos, magazines, instruments and other trinkets. The collage reflected the pair's tastes in fashion, music, TV and film, comedy, politics, literature and, in Mick's case, sport.

Whereas *Café Bleu* felt like a lucky dip into Weller's varied musical tastes, *Our Favourite Shop* forged these flavours into a more cohesive sound – which was odd, bearing in mind the involvement of over twenty 'Honorary Councillors'. The most notable of these musicians were Camelle Hinds, who was now their unofficial bassist, and Dee C. Lee, who sang on six songs. The other acute difference between the LPs was *Our Favourite Shop*'s absence of jazz influences, aside from the occasional guitar lick or Latin groove.

Over half the lyrics were of a clear-cut political persuasion, making it Weller's boldest statement of intent to date, supported on the cover by quotes from outspoken intellectual and Labour MP Tony Benn, radical US comedian Lenny Bruce and Oscar Wilde's *Man Under Socialism*. In hindsight, *Our Favourite Shop* represented the pinnacle of Paul's use of overtly political sentiments in music. Thankfully, though, the songs weren't tarred with a staunch party-political brush, and while a few dealt with specific issues, many lyrics painted broader strokes.

HOMEBREAKERS

The album's opener – one of four Weller/Talbot compositions – eloquently highlighted the plight of a family ripped apart by unemployment and poverty, though Talbot's vocal lacked the depth of character of Weller's.

ALL GONE AWAY

One of the album's musically softer moments reflected the regret of this paean to what Weller saw as a break-down in society at the expense of Eighties corporate greed. Again, the breezy, almost bossa nova beat only sharpens the song's message. 'Clark Kent' of swing-jazz act The Chevalier Brothers played 'contra' bass.

COME TO MILTON KEYNES

One of the LP's least convincing ventures was this unprovoked attack on the Bedfordshire 'new town' notorious for its faceless linear plan and 'artificial' architecture. The song's lyrics suggested a reality of drugs, violence and "losing our way" behind a facade of "luscious houses", where the "curtains are drawn", the idea being to create a musical pastiche which matched the supposed artificiality of Milton Keynes itself. "Every piece of tackiness we could think of was thrown in," commented Paul, explaining its quirky mix of horns and strings and the snatches of the *Sale Of The Century* theme, 'Viva Espana!', 'Robin Hood' and a cricket commentary voice.

'Come To Milton Keynes' was banned from some TV and radio stations after complaints from enraged local residents. The adverse reaction was wholly justified: not only had Weller never visited Milton Keynes, but the town's similarities with Woking, by then a booming Eighties equivalent of a 'new town' itself, were considerable. Woking, therefore, might have made for a more logical target – but the songwriter chose not to soil his own doorstep.

To add insult to injury, 'Come To Milton Keynes' was chosen as the band's next single at the end of June. The Style Council had made their first significant mistake – and one of the weakest possible selections from *Our Favourite Shop* was their first single to miss the Top 20. Within a few weeks, Weller confessed his regret about the decision. An exclusive instrumental mix was donated to a compilation album, *Sons Of Jobs For*

The Boys, aimed at raising awareness about unemployment on Merseyside – so at least something productive came of the song.

INTERNATIONALISTS

Weller and Talbot also collaborated on one of the LP's cornerstones, using a variation on the Modernist/Stylist terminology to suggest, as Paul put it, "someone who doesn't identify strictly with their own country". Powered by Weller's wah-wah guitar, this urgent soul-rock workout updated the theme of The Jam's "Trans-Global Express" by reiterating the need for worldwide unity and, ultimately, some form of revolution to somehow rid the world of inequality. "A song about the power we all possess if we choose to unite and rise up to fight capitalism and oppression," was how Paul summarised it, with an idealistic naïvety. "I thought of the old socialist song, 'The Internationale'."

A STONE'S THROW AWAY

Weller's evocative ode to the universal nature of struggle was dramatised to great effect by its naked string orchestration, which made for one of the album's must haunting moments.

THE STAND UP COMIC'S INSTRUCTIONS

The album's main pitfall was this unfortunate experiment with comedian Lenny Henry, whom the band had met on several occasions, both on his various TV shows over the years (he sang 'You're The Best Thing' with them on an episode of TV's *Saturday Live*) and via his work with the International Year of Youth. Lenny's rap on 'The Stand Up Comic's Instructions' mimicked the racist bigotry of Northern comedians – the twist, of course, being that Lenny is black – but the song's novelty rapidly wore off.

BOY WHO CRIED WOLF

'Boy Who Cried Wolf' was issued throughout the rest of the world, where Milton Keynes held no significance, as the second single from *Our Favourite Shop*. Despite some now-dated synth sounds and an insensitive production, the song's plaintive melody carried it through, helped by backing vocals from Tracie.

A MAN OF GREAT PROMISE

The album's real gem was Paul's heartfelt memorial to his old school friend Dave Waller, which had been premiered during the band's 'Council Meetings Part Two' concerts in autumn 1984. Back in 1978, in the songbook for The Jam's *All Mod Cons*, Weller had included a tribute to his friend: "Dave, your words fill me with new hope for the modern world, whilst your words on decay and destruction have the foresight of a person a 1,000 years old. There are those who are held in high esteem who do not deserve it in light of you." The letter was signed "Your loyal and devoted friend, Weller P. (fan club No. 0001)". Weller had pondered over releasing 'Man Of Great Promise' as a single but decided against it – maybe he was too emotionally bound up with its subject matter.

DOWN IN THE SEINE

Equally beguiling was 'Down In The Seine', described by Talbot as an "aggressive, European-flavoured waltz", and inspired by Scott Walker's interpretations of Belgian *chansonnier* Jacques Brel.

THE LODGERS (OR SHE WAS ONLY A SHOPKEEPER'S DAUGHTER)

The theme of another Weller/Talbot song was evident from its subtitle – the lodgers in question being the Conservative Party, of course. This was one of Weller's first serious attempts at writing a modern soul tune, an ideal vehicle as the backdrop for another anti-Government tirade.

The song was re-recorded as the follow-up to 'Milton Keynes'. But 'The Lodgers' had already been given a 'Club Mix' on the 12" of 'Milton Keynes'. Four months after the album's release, the band expected their fans to accept a third variation as their new single with the caption, "presented to you by public demand". Admittedly, it sounded more robust, with the addition of a horn section (and Camille Hinds' bass in place of the original synth). But an absence of new songs was masked by twenty minutes of live recordings from their summer tour.

Dee C. Lee featured prominently on the single, receiving a full credit for the first time and appearing next to Paul and Mick on the cover photo backstage after performing on Channel 4's *Soul Train*. Soon afterwards, Weller's romantic involvement with Dee was made public.

LUCK

At the other end of the spectrum to the earnest funk-rock of 'Internationalists' was the final Talbot-Weller creation on the album, 'Luck', a bouncy pop ditty which evoked summery images. This upbeat feel was perfectly suited to its theme of new love/friendship.

WITH EVERYTHING TO LOSE

Some of the album's most unsettling lyrics were accompanied by its softest music. After learning about the plight of those who had died on YTS schemes, Steve White wrote new lyrics for Weller's 'Have You Ever Had It Blue?' (which had then yet to be released). The result, 'With Everything To Lose', portrayed a sadness amplified by a mournful melody.

OUR FAVOURITE SHOP

One of Mick's funkiest instrumentals was chosen as the title track, later reworked to great effect on the 12" of 'Come To Milton Keynes'. Its Latin Jazz flavour represented one of the few direct links with *Café Bleu*.

WALLS COME TUMBLING DOWN!

To those fans who had grown disillusioned with The Style Council's tuneful ballads or the eclecticism of *Café Bleu*, this single felt like a warrior returning. There was no ambiguity here, aside from the bizarre sight on the sepia-toned front cover of a pouting Mick Talbot wearing make-up à la Buster Keaton.

"You don't have to take this crap," Weller barked gruffly, above a solid, Northern Soul bedrock of horns, organ and a driving beat. "You don't have to sit back and Relax". The last word alluded to the 'Frankie Say Relax' T-shirt craze which followed the enormous success of Frankie Goes To Hollywood's single a year or so earlier. Succinct and hard-hitting, 'Walls Come Tumbling Down' also took a pot-shot at the "public enemies No. 10", with a revolutionary cry which preached that "we can actually try changing things".

NON-ALBUM SONGS

THE WHOLE POINT II

The B-sides to 'Walls Come Tumbling Down', credited to the Council Folk Club, began with 'The Whole Point II', which succinctly expanded upon the anti-"lords and ladies" message of that late addition to *Café Bleu*.

BLOOD SPORTS

This disdain for the upper classes continued with the second B-side, the acoustic 'Blood Sports', a scathing attack on hunting which was written for a fund-raising compilation album. The song's songwriting royalties were donated to a defence fund for two members of the Hunt Saboteurs Association, who were being held in remand for anti-blood sport activities.

SPIN' DRIFTING

The scent of a summer breeze pervaded this buoyant B-side, which followed in stark contrast to 'Walls Come Tumbling Down'. The lyrics seemed to suggest, in poetic manner, fading love and regret: "I was hoping to be found alive/In a pool of regret and an ocean of tears", but the music shared the uplifting, Continental feeling of the Council's earlier Parisian sessions.

(WHEN YOU) CALL ME

A more sensible choice than the beleaguered 'Come To Milton Keynes' might have been its B-side, '(When You) Call Me', a simple, gospel-tinged love song marred only by a heavy-handed synth drum. The song was later covered as a single by Tracie, having earlier been offered to ex-Love Affair singer Steve Ellis.

HAVE YOU EVER HAD IT BLUE?

This breezy, Latin-styled song had been written for a film adaptation of *Absolute Beginners*. It was first aired during Style Council concerts in autumn 1984 but wasn't issued as a single until spring 1986; the lyrics had been rewritten in the meantime for Steve White's 'With Everything To Lose'.

'Have You Ever Had It Blue?' had a jazzy, tropical flavour and wistful lyrics, which suited the soundtrack to Julien Temple's stylised (and ill-fated) musical adaptation of Colin MacInnes's vivid tale of late Fifties London. As it transpired, only a few bars were heard in the movie, much to Paul's exasperation; there had been talk of him scoring the whole movie. The single was a Top 20 hit, though, and the film's dancers, The Jazz Defektors, performed in the accompanying video.

MR. COOL'S DREAM

The Style Council's other contribution to the *Absolute Beginners* soundtrack was Mick Talbot's laid-back jazz instrumental, which backed 'Have You Ever Had It Blue?' The subtle arrangement came courtesy of jazz legend Gil Evans.

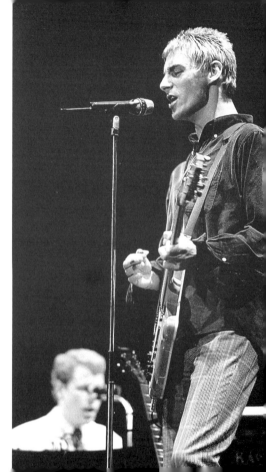

THE COST OF LOVING

THE COST OF LOVING

DATE: FEBRUARY 1987

CHART POSITION: NO. 2

ORIGINAL LP: TSCLP 4

CURRENT CD: POLYDOR 831 443-2

In September 1986, The Style Council performed two new songs, 'It Didn't Matter' and 'Angel', on a TV special, *Rock Around The Dock*, staged on the river Mersey. The most striking aspect about both tunes was the backing music, which mimicked the glossy, sophisticated production of contemporary American soul. It was obvious that Dee C. Lee's tastes were rubbing off on Paul.

Chosen as the next Style Council single, 'It Didn't Matter' was universally trounced by critics. Outside of specialist soul publications, few journalists were sympathetic to the sounds of the U.S. R&B charts – let alone Weller's clumsy attempts at emulating them – and leading American soul artists like Luther Vandross, Freddie Jackson and Alexander O'Neal received scant attention from the white press.

The same indifference greeted the band's new LP, *The Cost Of Loving*, in February – and with some justification. Packaged as a DJ-friendly double pack which played at 45rpm, it contained only nine tracks, allegedly because they tended to be longer than before. (Many of the out-takes finally surfaced on the rarities CD, *Here's Some That Got Away*.) The album suffered from a crisp, antiseptic feel, the result of Weller's single-handed production. There was little of the earthiness or energy of their earlier records and Talbot had dropped the electric organ – a key ingredient of the band's earlier musical brew – for the cleaner sound of the Rhodes piano and synthesiser. And the undiluted enthusiasm which had accompanied *Our Favourite*

Shop was absent. Some of the songs were excellent, though: 'Fairy Tales', 'Right To Go', 'Heavens Above!', 'Waiting' and 'The Cost Of Loving' itself. The problems lay with the slower songs, which congregated on the second disc. 'Walking The Night' and Anita Baker's 'Angel' were sickly smooth.

Collectively, then, the album felt bitty and incomplete. This was unfortunate because the band patently considered the LP as a whole, rather than as individual components – and they dithered over which songs should be chosen as singles. 'It Didn't Matter' had been a last-minute choice and while the title track was issued in Japan and 'Heavens Above!' came out in America, Britain were dealt the graceful but uncommercial ballad, 'Waiting'.

The LP's most striking aspect was its anonymous plain orange sleeve, which featured merely the album title and the band's initials, both barely legible. It was Weller's 'Orange Album' in the style of The Beatles' 'White Album' – much to Polydor's consternation. Weller commented

that "I like music with bollocks" but *The Cost Of Loving* had nothing much swinging between its legs. Nor was it that successful: despite reaching a respectable No. 2, the album quickly fell out the charts. Weller was playing into the cynics' hands: for all his efforts at injecting some humour into his image and his music, *The Cost Of Loving* sounded like the product of someone taking himself too seriously.

IT DIDN'T MATTER

When the minimal, laid-back groove of 'It Didn't Matter' was released as the first Style Council single of 1987, it was a disappointment. Weller's voice sounded hollow and disinterested, and the sterile backing music was flat and dreary, which wasn't helped by the song's lumpish rhythm. In trying to recreate the high-tech production values of cutting-edge American soul, as created by backroom boys like Jimmy Jam & Terry Lewis and a host of under-ground names, Weller ended up with a bland production which lacked the character and melodic strength of previous ballads like 'Long Hot Summer' and 'You're The Best Thing'.

RIGHT TO GO

'Right To Go' was an effective hip-hop track featuring a young London rap trio, the Dynamic Three, which picked up where 'A Gospel' had left off in 1984. The song's original title, 'The Right Must Go', spelt out the song's message more clearly – and the lyrics urged people to register to vote in the forthcoming general election.

HEAVENS ABOVE

The majestic 'Heavens Above!' resurrected the spirit of early Seventies Marvin Gaye (especially *What's Going On*). Its soaring melody and gliding rhythm which moved up a gear halfway through, breaking into an infectious jazz-funk jam.

FAIRY TALES

'Fairy Tales' set an anti-Thatcher lyric — one of Paul's last directly party political tirades — to a beefy R&B rhythm fuelled by a six-piece horn section and percussion from TSC regular Steve Sidelnyk (now with Massive Attack).

ANGEL

This soaring ballad made no effort to alter its original performance by one of America's leading soul singers, Anita Baker. But Dee was no match for Baker and this atmospheric love song sounded brittle in the hands of The Style Council.

WALKING THE NIGHT

The elegant jazz-soul of 'Walking The Night' featured backing vocals from John Valentine of The Valentine Brothers, whose most famous song, 'Money's Too Tight To Mention', had given Simply Red their first hit.

WAITING

This may have been one of the LP's genuine highlights but as a single, it flopped: issued in March 1987, 'Waiting' was the first Style Council 45 to evade the Top 40. Something was definitely amiss.

THE COST OF LOVING

The title track of the album succeeded where others failed, melding a crisp, mellow slow backbeat to a sublime, dreamy melody that oozed soul – and Weller's voice, for once, suited the tune. The song was re-recorded for the B-side of 'Wanted', a much slower reworking which had been commissioned for Lezli-An Barrett's well-received motion picture, *Business As Usual*, a pro-union/anti-Thatcherite drama starring Glenda Jackson, Cathy Tyson and John Thaw.

A WOMAN'S SONG

Less grating than many of the album's ballads was 'A Woman's Song', which was added at the last moment (the song wasn't listed on the sleeve). This ornate creation was based around an old nursery rhyme, but Dee C. Lee's vocal on this and other songs occasionally sounded brittle at times.

NON-ALBUM SONGS

ALL YEAR ROUND

The flipside of 'It Didn't Matter' was even weaker than its lead track, despite borrowing its tune from the far superior 'Big Boss Groove'.

FRANCOISE

One of the B-sides to 'Waiting', 'Francoise', was the delicate theme tune to The Style Council's ill-fated excursion into cinema. *Jerusalem* was a comic, ham-fisted exploration of the British condition, attempting to satirise our class system, as well as American imperialism and rock'n'roll clichés. But it fell way short of its aims.

WANTED

Issued in October '87 in the wake of *The Cost Of Loving*, 'Wanted' was subtitled 'Waiter, There's Some Soup In My Flies' in another bizarre attempt to bemuse the band's audience. As for the tune itself, this was a straightforward soul-pop ode to unrequited love, but its forlorn, yearning lyrics were disguised by its breezy melody. Still, the song had a more upbeat, endearing feel than most of *The Cost Of Loving*.

CONFESSIONS OF A POP GROUP

THE STYLE COUNCIL

NEW YORK · GSTAAD · TOKYO · MARBLE ARCH

CONFESSIONS OF A POP GROUP

DATE: JUNE 1988

CHART POSITION: NO. 15

ORIGINAL LP: TSCLP 5

CURRENT CD: POLYDOR 835 785-2

'Wanted' aside, The Style Council kept a low profile in the months leading up to what transpired to be their last album. All was quiet until the arrival of a bizarre, brashly-produced new single, 'Life At A Top People's Health Farm', in May 1988. The bare-chested, sun-tanned Weller and Talbot – thumbs up and wearing straw boaters – looked out from the sleeve with beaming grins as if to test people's patience.

Confessions Of A Pop Group arrived a month later. Clocking in at nearly an hour, this was by far The Style Council's longest album, and also their least understood. *The Cost Of Loving* may have flummoxed many people but it still very nearly topped the charts. *Confessions...*, by contrast, only reached No. 15 (their only LP not to make the Top 10), and vanished from the charts after just three weeks.

The album title followed 'Life At A Top People's Health Farm' (and that subtitle for 'Wanted') in a series of tongue-in-cheek names which seemed to confirm Weller's look of ennui on the cover. A sense of fun was evident from many of his lyrics, but they were sometimes interpreted as clever-clever. The combined effect of the refined music and Dan Davies' colourful fine art paintings, visually describing each song, was one of taste and sophistication. The band always acted as self-professed arbiters of style but maybe they had now taken the stance too far? Needless to say, the LP was less than favourably received by the critics.

Confessions... was quieter and more reflective than *The Cost Of Loving* – but though Paul's vocal technique had noticeably improved, there was none of that old Weller passion. The album was divided in two: the first side was subtitled 'The Piano Paintings', and over five compositions, the group dabbled in classical music with lush string arrangements, gentle melodies and a meandering atmosphere – all of which somehow recalled Brian Wilson's melancholy feel on the Beach Boys' classic *Pet Sounds*.

Put quite simply, *Confessions Of A Pop Group* was Weller's deepest, most complex album to date, with a breadth and diversity reflected by the wide range of instruments and guest musicians. The whole package seemed very grown-up – but then that wasn't altogether surprising. On the sleeve, Dee C. Lee was seen tactically positioned behind the piano to disguise the fact she was heavily pregnant. Dee and Paul had married in July 1987, and a month before the album's release in June 1988, she gave birth to a son, Nathaniel (known as Natty for short).

IT'S A VERY DEEP SEA

'It's A Very Deep Sea' was one of three new songs aired during the previous autumn's *Renaissance Tour*. This mournful lullaby possessed outwardly sad lyrics laced with regret and self-doubt – of "dredging up the past to drive me round the bendz" and "crying over nothing worth crying for". Strangely enough, bearing in mind its theme, the song was segued into The Beach Boys' 'California Girls' during the group's last show at the Royal Albert Hall.

THE STORY OF SOMEONE'S SHOE

One of the album's gems, 'The Story Of Someone's Shoe' dealt with the seedy emptiness of a one-night stand, a theme softened by vibraphone and the soothing harmonies of The Swingle Singers – "easy listening à la Michel Legrand", as Paul later described it, an influence which dated back to *Café Bleu*.

CHANGING OF THE GUARD

One of the most beautiful, contemplative moments on the album was this paean to Paul's past relationship with Gill Price. Laced with self-doubt and regret, the lyrics suggest second thoughts, as Paul and – ironically enough – Dee delivered their very best 'soul ballad' vocals.

THE LITTLE BOY IN A CASTLE

'The Little Boy In The Castle' was a delicate piano instrumental, the second section of which was subtitled 'A Dove Flew Down The Elephant' (as in the Elephant & Castle in South London). This chalk'n'cheese marriage of fairy tale imagery and everyday London life epitomised The Style Council circa '88.

THE GARDENER OF EDEN (A THREE PIECE SUITE)

Then there was an ambitious, ten-minute-plus composition in three parts: in the central section, 'The Gardener Of Eden' cast a weary eye over today's ecological ravages in one of Weller's most sensitive lyrics, set to a mesmerising jazz tune sung by Dee C. Lee. This was preceded by an ornate harpsichord piece, 'In The Beginning', and the 'Three Piece Suite' (as it was subtitled) ended with another of Talbot's quiet piano solos, 'Mourning The Passing Of Time'.

LIFE AT A TOP PEOPLE'S HEALTH FARM

Weller described this oddity as an update of Bob Dylan's mid-Sixties rant, 'Subterranean Homesick Blues'. True, it shared Dylan's ramshackle collage of names and ideas – the witty, punning lyrics name-dropped public figures as diverse as Margaret Thatcher, *The Archers* and Leon Trotsky with images of dog tracks, bingo, gas shares and lettuce. But its production was messy, the whining vocals drowned among a clatter of murky horns and crass drums. Weller was soon critical of the single, too: "I hate it," he admitted. "I listen to it now, a year later, and I can't think where I was at then."

WHY I WENT MISSING

Side two was more upbeat. Above a wonderfully warm melody, the gentle, soaring 'Why I Went Missing' sounded distinctly like a confessional – "There's plenty more I could have kissed/And those who wanted it – I could of resist/But I blamed myself for this out of town kissing".

HOW SHE THREW IT ALL AWAY

Just as charming was the jolly soul-pop of 'How She Threw It All Away' (with its shades of Earth, Wind And Fire's 'September'), helped by veteran jazzer Dick Morrissey on flute and drummer Nick Brown in place of Steve White. Again, Weller's old flame Gill Price

appears to be the subject in question. The song was sensibly chosen to lead off a post-album single, the *1-2-3-4* EP, subtitled 'A Summer Quartet'. But its relative lack of success reinforced the Council's waning commercial fortunes.

IWASADOLEDADSTOYBOY

The cheeky, tabloid-inspired wordplay of this ball of musical confusion reflected Weller's shift from political ideologist to social observer and even satirist. With shades of 'Life At A Top People's Health Farm', the lyrics again hinted at an increasingly bleak society.

CONFESSIONS 1, 2 & 3

This ponderous ballad had been one of three new songs aired during the previous autumn's *Renaissance Tour*, with more than a hint of the atmosphere of Elvis Costello's *Shipbuilding*. Again, the subject seemed to be an old flame, the line, "Take it away get your lawyer involved", reinforcing rumours of out-of-court settlements…

CONFESSIONS OF A POP GROUP

The album's real masterpiece was the title track which ended the LP. Nearly ten minutes long, this impressionistic attack on decaying society was underpinned by an incredibly funky bassline – it felt like a slowed-down, more sophisticated 'Money-Go-Round'.

NON-ALBUM SONGS

SWEET LOVING WAYS

The flipside of 'Life At A Top People's Health Farm' was less abrasive: a beguiling, laid-back, jazz-soul love song with relaxed guitar playing reminiscent of George Benson.

LOVE THE FIRST TIME

'How She Threw It All Away' was followed by the sublime, bossa nova feel of 'Love The First Time', a pleasant, self-explanatory tribute to Weller's blossoming relationship with Dee C. Lee.

I DO LIKE TO BE B-SIDE THE A-SIDE

The *1-2-3-4* EP ended with this instrumental credited to the Mixed Campanions, an update of Talbot's *Mick's Company*. But it was a reflection of the band's fading fortunes that the EP stalled outside the Top 40.

THE STYLE COUNCIL MODERNISM: A NEW DECADE

A DECADE OF MODERNISM

SCHEDULED FOR SUMMER 1989
ORIGINAL LP: SCHEDULED TO BE TSCLP 6 BUT CANCELLED
CURRENT CD: FINAL DISC OF THE STYLE COUNCIL BOX SET

By early 1989, The Style Council were running short of ideas. Weller had fallen in love with the more soulful strands of Chicago House music that were dominating the more discerning club dancefloors. One of his favourite records of the period was Joe Smooth's classic House hit, 'Promised Land', a popular import before the single was given a full British release at the start of 1989. A few weeks later, in mid-February, The Style Council were performing their own version of 'Promised Land' on *Top Of The Pops*.

Despite reports that the next Style Council LP was to be titled *Modernism: A New Decade* (or *A Decade Of Modernism*, as the LP is sometimes known, or even *1990: A New Decade In Modernism*), the band were strangely silent. A scheduled single, 'Sure Is Sure' / 'Love Of The World', never materialised, and a press release was eventually circulated in August to announce that not only had both the LP and the single been scrapped, but that The Style Council, after six years, had disbanded. *Modernism: A New Decade* has since earned the tag of Weller's "great lost album", but needless to say, it lacked the musical ambition of other shelved projects such as *Lifehouse* (Pete Townshend) or *Smile* (Brian Wilson). The songs were devoid of Weller's usual trademarks – there was none of his lyrical bite or even the musical adventurism of *Confessions Of A Pop Group*. But he has always been able to replicate a particular genre – and as a club-derived soul/House LP, *Modernism: A New Decade* was a respectable effort.

Its most distinguishing characteristics were a synthetic, hi-tech House production (which made *The Cost Of Loving* sound positively analogue), and the lyrics, submerged as they were under a chunky House beat, relied on a simple gospel message of unity and love. "At the time, I really believed that Garage House was the new mod music," Paul later commented. Two of the songs were issued as B-sides; Weller returned to 'That Spiritual Feeling' on his first solo single; and 'Sure Is Sure' later surfaced on a bootleg EP. But the rest of the album didn't materialise until nearly a decade later on The Style Council box set, *The Complete Adventures*....

A NEW DECADE

The synthetic beats and overtly House production of *Modernism: A New Decade* kicked off with this instrumental dance outing, with an opening "Let's go!" from a Teddy Pendergrass soundalike to hang onto.

CAN YOU STILL LOVE ME?

'Can You Still Love Me?' was one of the few songs to be officially released – on

the flipside of 'Promised Land'. It sounded chunkier and more natural than its A-side, but still blatantly mimicked Chicago House with a melody not dissimilar to Colonel Abrams' massive mid-Eighties hit, 'Trapped' – itself an influence on House. The single was remixed by Juan Atkins of Model 500, a pioneer of Detroit's emergent techno House sound.

The album version was different inasmuch as Weller tackled the vocal, instead of the unnamed (and presumably black) soul singer heard on the single.

THE WORLD MUST COME TOGETHER

The unifying message of Chicago House seemed to Paul to hark back to the golden days of late Sixties/early Seventies soul – Marvin Gaye, Curtis Mayfield et al. But the empty (ecstasy-fuelled) hyperbole of most House music lacked the same conviction, a fact evinced when Paul was unable to remember some of the (indecipherable) lyrics to this song.

HOPE (FEELINGS GONNA GETCHA')

'Hope (Feelings Gonna Getcha')' was aired that summer after Weller gave an advance copy to a London DJ. The song was performed at The Style Council's live finale at the Royal Albert Hall.

THAT SPIRITUAL FEELING

Marco Nelson (a member of The Young Disciples who had played bass at their Albert Hall event and was later a main-stay on bass during Weller's solo career) took an advance copy of 'That Spiritual Feeling' down to Dingwalls, then North London's premier funk club in Camden Lock, where jazz DJ Gilles Peterson made a special announcement before playing it. Weller described this liaison with James Brown's old backing band The J.B.'s and girl duo Trouble And Bass both as "Hip-House" and "Jazz-Funk"; though a more suitable description might have been Acid Jazz. The track was later reworked on Weller's début solo single, 'Into Tomorrow'.

EVERYBODY'S ON THE RUN

This 'brand new track' was issued on the flipside of the '89 Mix' of 'Long Hot Summer', which Polydor used to publicise their 'Greatest Hits' album, *The Singular Adventures Of The Style Council*, earlier that year. It shared the Garage House vibe of 'Can You Still Love Me?' Mixed by New Yorker Freddie Bastone, alias House outfit Corporation Of One (responsible for the club favourite, 'The Real Life'), the song featured guest soul vocalist Brian J. Powell.

LOVE OF THE WORLD

No lesser musical heavyweight than journalist Paolo Hewitt appears to have guested as vocalist on 'Love Of The World'. The "Amore del mondo" chant (with shades of Ibiza) and "the bigger the mountain, the higher the climb" were blatant House techniques – as was the title itself, which formed the basis of the chorus. One word: ecstasy (even though the pair had reportedly never dabbled in the drug at this point).

SURE IS SURE

The Style Council's last single was scrapped along with the album. But 'Sure Is Sure' was one of the most fully-formed 'songs', its typically House-styled call for unity fleshed out with a traditional verse/chorus/verse structure, rather than the mantra-like nature of the rest of the album. The band performed the song when they reunited for a brief, one-off live set for Japanese satellite TV in spring 1990.

NON-ALBUM SONGS

PROMISED LAND

Weller's decision to plagiarise a contemporary House record remains one of the most bizarre of his career – it was probably due to a combination of impulse, boredom and a genuine love of the tune itself.

"I just thought it was a good song," Paul explained. "It always sounded like a gospel song to me, the chords and the voices. We didn't change it that much really, we just made it more inspira-tional, more up." If the House beat was stripped away, 'Promised Land' shared the spiritual soul vibe of Curtis Mayfield's 'Move On Up'. But by opting for such a derivative rhythm, The Style Council added little to Joe Smooth's original treatment.

The Style Council were resolutely criticised in leading dance/soul magazines. To cynics of Weller's recent conversion to House, it felt like he was cashing in. Nevertheless, the single sold well through specialist dance shops and was played on soul radio stations – and since Garage House was still an underground phenomenon, these were usually the illegal ones, a fact which impressed its creator.

THE STYLE COUNCIL

HERE'S SOME THAT GOT AWAY

Contains Rare & Unreleased Recordings

HERE'S SOME THAT GOT AWAY

DATE: JUNE 1993
CHART POSITION: NO. 39
ORIGINAL CD: POLYDOR 519 372-2

In the wake of the success of The Jam's *Extras* album, which combined stray B-sides with previously unheard studio demos and out-takes, Polydor followed suit with this assemblage of Style Council rarities. Because the majority of the early Style Council recordings were released on singles, most of these discoveries dated from 1986 onwards, from the sessions around *The Cost Of Loving* and *Confessions Of A Pop Group*.

LOVE PAINS/NIGHT AFTER NIGHT

Weller's immersion in modern soul was reflected in these two previously unissued cover versions of contemporary independent club hits from 1986. 'Love Pains' was a Willie Clayton track, which Weller managed to tackle in surprisingly soulful fashion; less impressive was the more laid-back 'Night After Night' by David Sea, the rhythm of which was borrowed for The Style Council's last significant hit, 'It Didn't Matter'.

A CASUAL AFFAIR

Recorded in 1985, this presumably dates from the sessions for *Our Favourite Shop*, and its wayward vocal about a love on the rocks might well have tallied with Paul's fragmenting relationship with Gill Price, with lines like: "Memories rearrange themselves to misery for me". It's pleasant enough, but Weller was probably right to leave it in the vault at the time.

WAITING ON A CONNECTION

The album's most vital discovery, 'Waiting On A Connection' was a vibrant modern soul tune recorded in 1988 for North London funk band Push, due to Paul's involvement with the Acid Jazz scene. But the song was shelved – a great pity, in hindsight, because Paul's convincing vocal was perfectly offset by its polished, sassy production and a wonderful funk hook.

MY VERY GOOD FRIEND

Defiantly Eighties keyboards dominated this upfront funk number, making it sound like an excerpt from *The Kids From 'Fame'*, despite some attractive percussion. The song itself was a pleasant ode to a new flame – and since it was recorded in 1986, that was probably Dee C. Lee.

APRIL'S FOOL

The smell of satin sheets and champagne glasses oozed from this sultry jazz-soul ballad from 1986, perfect in the hands of Al Jarreau or Anita Baker but painful when crooned by Weller. That motto about oil and water springs to mind…

WHO WILL BUY

More interesting was a tender performance of Lionel Bart's 'Who Will Buy' (from his Sixties musical adaptation of *Oliver!*), which had been restricted to the Japanese B-side of 'It Didn't Matter'. In other words, this presumably dated from the sessions for *The Cost Of Loving*.

I AIN'T GOIN' UNDER

Another of the true finds on *Here's Some That Got Away* was this gritty street-funk original penned for comedian Lenny Henry to record in the wake of 'A Stand-Up Comic's Instructions', his contribution to *Our Favourite Shop*. The

Style Council recorded their version in 1986, complete with some stunning fuzz funk guitar – and *The Cost Of Loving* would have been a far better record with its inclusion.

I AM LEAVING

Dee C. Lee sang on this hitherto unheard, Chaka Khan-influenced Weller original, a tepid modern soul tune spoilt by antiseptic Eighties synths.

A WOMAN'S SONG (Demo)/A STONE'S THROW AWAY (Demo)

Both these songs were low-key dry-runs featuring just Paul and Mick. 'A Woman's Song' appeared on *The Cost Of Loving* (Paul sings here, instead of Dee); though the liner notes date this version as being recorded in 1988, a year after the album. And 'A Stone's Throw Away' is a template for one of the highlights of *Our Favourite Shop.*

The other songs had already been issued as B-sides: 'Party Chambers', 'The Whole Point II', 'The Ghosts Of Dachau', 'Sweet Loving Ways', 'Mick's Up', 'The Piccadilly Trail', '(When You) Call Me', 'In Love For The First Time', 'Big Boss Groove', 'Mick's Company', 'Bloodsports'.

THE STYLE COUNCIL LIVE

The Style Council's early live appearances were a near-disaster. Without a steady line-up, the band couldn't gel together and the first, tentative performances were limited to just a handful of ramshackle songs (with rumours that backing tapes were used). Weller consciously avoided the temptation to tour, still smarting from the rigorous live schedule endured during his days with The Jam. The group's first 'Council Meetings' were abroad; their first live video was shot in Japan; and it was a year before The Council played their first British tour.

Once in full swing, though, the band were able to create an upbeat, party atmosphere that would have been impossible with The Jam. Free from the confines of the guitar, Weller was able to concentrate on singing and, on a good night, they could be a truly uplifting (perhaps even spiritual) experience. Sadly, little of these qualities was ever captured for posterity — excepting the *Far East And Far Out* video.

LIVE!
THE
STYLE
COUNCIL,
HOME &
ABROAD.

829 143-2

the style council IN CONCERT

PAUL WELLER MICK TALBOT DEE C. LEE STEVE WHITE

HOME & ABROAD

DATE: MAY 1986, NO. 8
ORIGINAL LP: TSCLP 3
CURRENT CD: POLYDOR 829 143-2

To bridge the gap between *Our Favourite Shop* and *The Cost Of Loving*, The Style Council concocted a live album, taken from their recent world tour. It reflected their more intensive touring schedule (remember they avoided playing live during their first year of existence). But the performances weren't a patch on those heard in the *Far East And Far Out* video (from 1984) and the band were obliged to overdub the music to bring it up to scratch. Also, an opportunity to include live tracks which had no studio counterparts was sorely missed.

The track listing was as follows:
'My Ever Changing Moods' / 'The Lodgers' / 'Headstart For Happiness' / '(When You) Call Me' / 'The Whole Point Of No Return' / 'With Everything To Lose' / 'Homebreakers' / 'Shout To The Top' / 'Walls Come Tumbling Down!' / 'Internationalists' / 'The Big Boss Groove' / 'Our Favourite Shop'

THE STYLE COUNCIL IN CONCERT

DATE: JANUARY 1998
CURRENT CD: POLYDOR 533 143-2

In essence, this was what *Home & Abroad* should have been: a comprehensive picture of the band's 'Council Meetings', with a healthy dose of songs unavailable elsewhere. *In Concert* was delayed for two years, eventually emerging in early 1998.

The full track listing was as follows:
'Meetin' (Over) Up Yonder' / 'Up For Grabs' / 'Long Hot Summer' / 'One Nation Under A Groove' / 'Le Départ' / 'Spring, Summer, Autumn' / 'Hangin' On To A Memory' / 'It Just Came To Pieces In My Hands' / 'Here's One That Got Away' / 'My Ever Changing Moods' / 'Man Of Great Promise' / 'Boy Who Cried Wolf' / 'A Stone's Throw Away' / 'Speak Like A Child' / 'Mick's Up' / 'You're The Best Thing' / 'Move On Up' / 'Down In The Seine' / 'It's A Very Deep Sea' / 'Heavens Above'

The following were songs unavailable in any form by The Style Council elsewhere:

MEETIN' (OVER) UP YONDER

Curtis Mayfield's late-Sixties anthem for The Impressions (a precursor to 'Move On Up', if ever there was one) was treated with the respect it deserved.

UP FOR GRABS

One of the songs aired during concerts in late 1983 was 'Up For Grabs', written about Sixties playwright Joe Orton – Paul had cited John Lahr's Orton biography, *Prick Up Your Ears*, as one of his favourite books. This song had been slated for inclusion on the 'My Ever Changing Moods' single, but a studio recording never materialised.

ONE NATION UNDER A GROOVE

This late Seventies' Funkadelic classic was a staple of clubland right through the 1980s, though The Style Council struggled to do the track justice.

HANGIN' ON TO A MEMORY

Paul and Mick were both huge fans of Invictus early Seventies soul act Chairmen Of The Board, the main vehicle for Holland-Dozier-Holland after they left Motown. They eventually ended up working with the band in 1986; and covered one of their funkiest songs, 'Hangin' On To A Memory', though Dee's vocal was a tad overpowering.

NON-ALBUM LIVE SONGS

IT JUST CAME TO PIECES IN MY HANDS
(Coventry)

SPEAK LIKE A CHILD
(London)

These poor quality recordings were pressed up on a live fanclub flexidisc to "bootleg the bootleggers". (CHECK LIVE LP).

MY EVER CHANGING MOODS
(Liverpool June 1985)

1985 may have represented The Style Council at their live peak; and several official recordings exist from this time, including this contribution to the *NME*'s *Drastic Plastic* EP.

WALLS COME TUMBLING DOWN!
(Manchester Apollo, June 14, 1985)

This graced the *Red Hot EP* given away with the first issue of *The Hit* magazine, which depicted Weller on the front cover dressed in boxing clobber.

LONG HOT SUMMER/ (WHEN YOU) CALL ME /INTERNATIONALISTS
(Sports & Entertainment Centre, Melbourne, Australia, August 18, 1985)

Paul Weller had never set foot on Antipodean soil before touring with The Style Council in summer '85. That was the location for some ugly business with his soon-to-be ex-girlfriend Gill Price. But the dates also threw up this exclusive live single.

LUCK

A live version of this breezy selection from *Our Favourite Shop* appeared on Dee C. Lee's hit single, 'See The Day'.

YOU'RE THE BEST THING/THE BIG BOSS GROOVE/MOVE ON UP/Medley: MONEY-GO-ROUND—SOUL DEEP—STRENGTH OF YOUR NATURE

(Liverpool & Manchester, 1985)

Prior to the release of *Home & Abroad*, the Style Council's principal concert recordings had been restricted to various formats of their summer '85 single, 'The Lodgers'. Curtis Mayfield's 'Move On Up' was a find; the track had been a favourite of Weller's since his days in The Jam.

WITH EVERYTHING TO LOSE

(Live In London Dec.ember 1985)

This highlight of *Our Favourite Shop* was tucked away on a cassette free with initial copies of the spring 1986 single, 'Have You Ever Had It Blue?'.

the singular adventures of the style council

GREATEST HITS VOL. 1

THE STYLE COUNCIL: COMPILATION ALBUMS

THE SINGULAR ADVENTURES OF THE STYLE COUNCIL (GREATEST HITS VOL. 1)

DATE: MARCH 1989
ORIGINAL LP: POLYDOR TSCTV 1
CURRENT CD: POLYDOR 837 896-2

As The Style Council's contemporary record sales waned, Polydor opted for a safe 'greatest hits' package of all their singles to date (minus the contentious 'Come To Milton Keynes'). But the lack of chronological order created a schizophrenic atmosphere. The CD edition sported 'Alternate Mixes' of 'You're The Best Thing' and 'The Lodgers' and 12" versions of 'Money-Go-Round', 'Have You Ever Had It Blue', 'My Ever Changing Moods' and 'Long Hot Summer 89'. These were missing from the vinyl edition – as were the two flops, 'How She Threw It All Away' and 'Waiting'.

HEADSTART FOR HAPPINESS – THE STYLE COUNCIL COLLECTION

DATE: OCTOBER 1991
ORIGINAL CD: PICKWICK PWKS 4090P

Whoever dreamed up this dreadful budget compilation seemed to have no idea about The Style Council's music, though the songs – with several glaring exceptions – represent the more melodic side of Weller's songwriting.

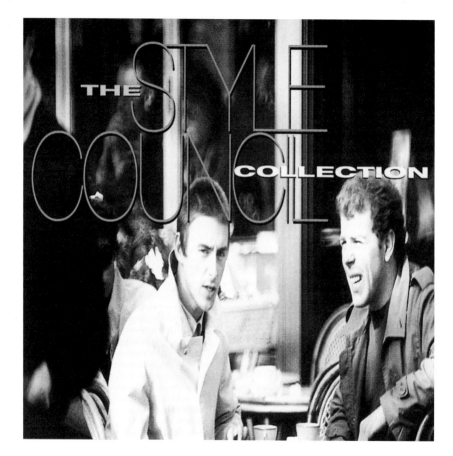

THE STYLE COUNCIL COLLECTION

DATE: MARCH 1996

ORIGINAL CD: POLYDOR 529 483-2

A more worthwhile exercise was this companion volume to *The Jam Collection*, though this Style Council equivalent did opt for several singles within the chronological track listing, as well as B-sides and album favourites. As such, it overlapped rather unnecessarily with *The Singular Adventures*…

KING TRUMAN
LIKE A GUN

One of the strangest releases of Weller's career was this anonymous-looking 12", issued on the then-hip Acid Jazz label in early 1989. 'Like A Gun' was strongly influenced by the wigged-out 1970s funk of Parliament/Funkadelic, its closest cousin in The Style Council being the title track to *Confessions Of A Pop Group*. But why disguise it? The song would have sounded as fitting on *Modernism: A New Decade* as 'That Spiritual Feeling'. Whatever the reasoning, the idea backfired: Acid Jazz had to hastily to withdraw the single after rumours of King Truman's true identity filtered through to Polydor.

slamslam

free your feelings

SLAM SLAM

FREE YOUR FEELINGS

DATE: APRIL 1991
ORIGINAL LP: MCA MCA 10147
CURRENT CD: MCA CDMCA 10147

During late 1989/early 1990, Paul Weller was genuinely unsure about his own career for the first time in his life — with no band or record label to fall back on. Instead, he busied himself helping out with his wife's new album, under the collective name of Slam Slam, together with friends Dr. Robert (from The Blow Monkeys) and Marco Nelson (who had by now formed the Young Disciples). The project evolved out of plans for a Dee C. Lee solo album (first mentioned in mid-1987).

Slam Slam's *Free Your Feelings* was a typical dance record of the period, with mechanical rhythms and synthesised drum patterns, but seven of the ten songs were either written or co-written by Weller. Originally available on import but finally issued in Britain in spring 1991, the LP shed some light on that farewell Style Council concert, which had premiered four of the songs: 'You'll Find Love' and 'Tender Love' (both penned by Paul), 'Move (Dance All Night)' (a joint effort between Dr. Robert and Dee C. Lee) and Dr. Robert's 'Depth Charge'.

The Slam Slam album represented a fascinating yet uncomfortable stop-gap between The Style Council and Paul's solo career. Had *Modernism: A New Decade* been released, then *Free Your Feelings* would have been its logical successor. Instead, the LP crystallised the problems Weller was facing in making the difficult transition from a musical dead-end to his eventual solo comeback. He tellingly spoke of the record as having happened "without point or reason". It showed.

Paul was credited with the following songs:

YOU'LL FIND LOVE/TENDER LOVE/GIVING IT UP/SOMETHING AIN'T RIGHT

Four Weller compositions, the last of which was Slam Slam's first single, issued in September 1990 many months before the album.

WHAT DREAMS ARE MADE OF

A co-composition between Weller and Mick Talbot.

NOTHING LIKE IT

This was one of the few tracks on which Paul collaborated with Dee C. Lee.

ROUND AND ROUND

Most significant of all was Paul's dreamy jazz-funk number, 'Round And Round' – simply because it would later surface in a reworked form on his first solo LP.

The other songs were: 'Move (Dance All Night)', 'Free Your Feelings' and 'Depth Charge'.

PAUL WELLER: STUDIO ALBUMS

PAUL WELLER

DATE: SEPTEMBER 1992
CHART POSITION: NO. 8
ORIGINAL LP/CD: GO! DISCS 828 343-1/2
CURRENT CD: ISLAND 828 355-2

There's a common misconception that Paul Weller disappeared from the music scene for several years. In fact, his return from the wilderness was slow but steady: he was back on the road within sixteen months of that ill-fated Style Council finale (and only six months on from a one-off TV reunion); and had a solo single out within two years of that remix of 'Long Hot Summer'. To his hardcore following (which probably constitutes some 100,000 fans in Britain alone), the break was shorter than most artists spend between albums. But his wider audience had drifted away after *The Cost Of Loving* in 1987 and wouldn't return until 1993's *Wild Wood* LP – a recess of over half a decade which would eventually culminate in the million-selling success of *Stanley Road*.

In the wake of a tentative tour in late 1990 billed as 'The Paul Weller Movement', Weller plugged away at his Solid Bond Studios as usual, recording various demos in the back room. Meanwhile, Marco Nelson's Young Disciples were in the main studio putting the finishing touches to their début album, a melting pot of soul, jazz and rap entitled *Road To Freedom* – and it was a fusion which captivated Paul.

Eventually, Weller developed some material that had real potential. Best of all was 'Into Tomorrow', a defiantly forward-thinking lyric ironically backed by music which wouldn't have sounded out of place on a late-Sixties Small Faces album. Paul was evidently going back to his roots, from the outwardly Mod target on the cover to the music within; and what was left of his audience welcomed the single with wide open arms, giving him a Top 40 single despite it being issued on his own independent label, Freedom High.

Unhappy with his band, Paul swiftly dispensed with most of 'The Movement', sticking only with drummer Steve White and flautist Jacko Peake to record his début album during late summer/autumn 1991. There was talk of a contract with Gilles Peterson's 'Acid Jazz' label Talkin' Loud, and an album, tentatively titled *SX 2000*, was slated for October. But a deal was eventually struck with Japanese label Pony Canyon and the LP, simply entitled *Paul Weller*, entered the Japanese International charts at No. 1 in late April 1992, staying there for over a month. *Paul Weller* was finally released in

Britain in September 1992 – behind the scenes, Weller had finally secured a UK record deal with Go! Discs.

The album was fanfared by Weller's next single, 'Uh Huh Oh Yeh', which put Weller back in the Top 20 for the first time in nearly five years. But his music was greeted with a surprisingly muted critical response – in fact, the LP was trounced by many reviewers, who considered it bland and directionless. Quite why is difficult to understand, since the album's music was as lavish as its packaging.

The doubters had overlooked a genuinely strong collection of songs. *Confessions*... had succeeded because of its sheer breadth and variety, but *Paul Weller* remains his strongest, most well-rounded collection of songs since *All Mod Cons*. Shades of The Style Council's soft soul were still evident. But the rest of the album was more stridently upbeat, musically if not lyrically – in fact, it contained some of Weller's most insightful and heartfelt lyrics. In short, *Paul Weller* was a masterpiece.

And it was an indication of the size and loyalty of Weller's audience that the album reached the Top 10.

UH HUH OH YEH

The album's opening track, 'Uh Huh Oh Yeh', preceded the LP as a single. The song began with a phased drum roll, a spacey mix of horns and a funky beat. Above this psychedelic vibe, Weller sang about his childhood in Woking, the first acknowledgement of his Surrey upbringing since 'Tales From The Riverbank'. The Jam song had been cryptic; 'Uh Huh Oh Yeh', on the other hand, made specific reference to the area around his old home. The first two lines, "I took a trip down Boundary Lane/Try an' find myself again", referred to Boundary Road, which is a couple of streets away from his old home in Stanley Road – indeed, the song's subject matter was emphasised by a promotional video shot on location in the back streets where he grew up.

It also suggested that, during that period of re-evaluation when his confidence had been shattered after the demise of The Style Council, his thoughts had taken him back to his youth. After Weller had spent most of his life relentlessly moving forward, disregarding his yesterdays – and the people involved in his yesterdays – he was now thinking, and writing, from a more reflective standpoint. One verse encapsulated his new state of mind: "And in my mind I saw the place/As each memory returned to trace/Dear reminders of who I am/The very roots upon which I stand."

Aside from its message, 'Uh Huh Oh Yeh' mined the same psychedelic funk-rock seam as 'Into Tomorrow', with stabs of sampled horns from an old Marsha Hunt song, 'Hot Rod Poppa' – it felt like a cross between, say, The Beatles' 'Strawberry Fields Forever' and The Small Faces' 'The Journey'.

I DIDN'T MEAN TO HURT YOU

The softly-spoken regret of tunes like 'I Didn't Mean To Hurt You' oozed the kind of bruised emotion that might roughly be defined as soul. Built around a similar backing track to 'Arrival Time', the song's lyrics may well have been linked to Paul's comment in the credits: "Thanks and love to Dee, my (fairly) long-standing and (frequently) long-suffering wife, who's stood by me when I've been way down and hateful for it, for putting up with my many moods..." It is fair to conclude that Paul Weller wasn't the easiest person with whom to live, during his soul-searching period of 1989 and 1990.

BULL-RUSH

The anthemic 'Bull-Rush' began with the lines, "In a momentary lapse of my condition/That sent me stumbling into a deep despair". But its Small Faces groove and melody's fresh, uplifting nature enlivened the mood before breaking out into a psychedelic end refrain borrowed from The Who's 'Magic Bus'. During the early months of 1993, 'Bull-Rush' was slated for single release but the idea was scrapped.

ROUND AND ROUND

A remake of this floating jazz-funk song from the Slam Slam LP was probably the album's only minor mistake, despite Weller's effort to beef the song up towards the end.

REMEMBER HOW WE STARTED

Hints of The Style Council's gliding soul melodies echoed through this angelic love song, a perfect example of how Paul's writing had made the transition from appearing disinterested to sounding truly heartfelt.

ABOVE THE CLOUDS

The mellow, Marvin Gaye-influenced groove of 'Above The Clouds' was issued as the second single from the album. It was an odd choice: the song's dreamy, soothing vibe lacked the commercial bite of songs like 'Bull-Rush' or even 'Clues', but maybe Paul wanted to counteract the upfront nature of 'Uh Huh Oh Yeh'. Co-produced by

Chris Bangs (of Acid Jazz and Galliano fame), the tune had a tranquil, summery atmosphere which might have caught the mood had it been issued earlier in the year. Instead, it clashed with the autumn mood of October and stalled outside the Top 40.

Again, the song's lyrics hinted at Weller's state of mind: "As my anger shouts/At my own self-doubt/So a sadness creeps/Into my dreams". When his inner emotions were expressed within Jam and Style Council songs, they tended to be externalised as anger against an outside entity. Confessions Of A Pop Group contained the first evidence of a more introspective side to his songwriting – and it's this aspect which dominated Paul Weller.

CLUES

In 'Clues', Weller sang about being, "Racked by my own self-doubt/I stumble and fall". But again, the moment of gloomy self-absorption was just one facet. 'Clues' was the album's most complex song instrumentally. The band often veered away from the strident melody to dabble into less structured passages, where Steve White's adventurous drumming bounced off Jacko Peake's swooping flute with a subtlety absent from Weller's more recent, post-Wild Wood work.

INTO TOMORROW

Snowed-in at Solid Bond Studios due to bad weather in the winter of 1990/1991, Weller and in-house engineer Brendan Lynch struck upon a novel mix of samples and beats to accompany one of Paul's most encouraging new songs, 'Into Tomorrow'. Paul produced it himself with Lynch's help, cutting the song live on Good Friday 1991 but retaining the guitar solo from the original demo, which had been played through a practice amp.

The Paul Weller Movement's 'Into Tomorrow' was issued on Freedom High in early May, the first evidence of the musician's reacquaintance with his guitar amp (and that demo also appeared on the single). The song's spacious production and its rhythmic mix of horns, organ and funky drums echoed late-Sixties acts like Julie Driscoll, Brian Auger & The Trinity. But its driving force was Weller's gutsy delivery – both in his passionate vocals and his vibrant guitar style. Its rough-and-ready edge had been conspicuous by its absence from Paul's music since mid-Eighties songs like 'Internationalists' and 'Walls Come Tumbling Down'. A backwards guitar solo even hinted at '66-era Beatles, which had so influenced Paul over a decade earlier.

AMONGST BUTTERFLIES

The strutting, folky soul groove of 'Amongst Butterflies' broke into a snatch from 'Arrival Time' as an inter-lude. Again, the lightness of touch of The Style Council had been reconfigured into an Acid Jazz-tinged funk pop sound (think Mother Earth).

THE STRANGE MUSEUM

One of the album's most haunting songs, 'The Strange Museum', had been previewed during Weller's first solo tour. Co-written with Mick Talbot (suggesting its vintage), this dreamy ballad was memorable not only for the capability of Weller's voice to carry the melody but also because of its vivid, mystical lyrics, all woven into a mellow, jazzy backcloth.

BITTERNESS RISING

Taking a leaf from the feel of Thunderclap Newman's old hit, 'Something In The Air', with a nod towards Curtis Mayfield, 'Bitterness Rising' was delivered like a catharsis: "Or the past will take you/Keep you from the truth/As bitterness rises/From the ashes of your youth". Meanwhile, the music grew from a pleasant R&B groove into an intense funk-rock brew. The same angst ran through much of the album. One of the major events was hidden in Paul's romantic credits: "This record is dedicated especially to Nathaniel and Leah – little arrows from our bow, may you soar high and always free." In October 1991, Dee had given birth to the couple's second child. But as his solo career took off, Paul had to make an unhappy compromise between the amount of time he devoted to his family and to his career.

KOSMOS

The album finished with another of the songs unveiled during those tentative early shows. 'Kosmos' was an experimental collage of funk and psychedelia with heaps of electronic effects from Brendan Lynch, as Weller chanted his quest for a sense of identity: "Who am I? What am I? Where am I to go?" The drums were lifted from an old P.P. Arnold tune and the soothing melody was pure Marvin Gaye. The result was an amalgam of *Sgt. Pepper* and *What's Going On* but from a Nineties perspective.

The song was the perfect vehicle for several (though arguably too many) overhauls by producer Brendan Lynch. The first, 'Kosmos SXDub 2000', accompanied 'Sunflower' on single, and the more radical 'Kosmos (Lynch Mob

Bonus Beats)' was tucked away on 'Hung Up'. Stripping most of the vocals away, Lynch used the dub techniques of echo and drop-out, adding eerie samples to create a psychedelic collage of sound.

NON-ALBUM SONGS

HERE'S A NEW THING

'Here's A New Thing' was one of the earliest songs to emerge from Weller's creative renaissance. The song was cut in 1991 with old Jam producer Pete Wilson, and was planned as a single. Weller drafted in a Cuban brass section and Steve White drummed along to sampled tape loops. The result was a jaunty, Latin soul number topped with horns and flute and built on a funky bassline and the piano riff from Marshall Jefferson's house classic, 'Move Your Body'. "The hardest thing is letting go/But once you do, life starts to flow," sang Weller in his best Curtis Mayfield falsetto, "Here's a new thing... Gotta let go of the past." If that 'past' referred to his skeleton-in-the-closet, The Jam,

then he had now stopped fighting against it.

THAT SPIRITUAL FEELING

The message was clear: Weller was striving forward. By the same token, he was also happy to resurrect 'That Spiritual Feeling' from 1989, a Style Council group composition with Talbot, Lee and Marco Nelson. This instrumental jazz-funk jam with James Brown's brass section, The J.B.'s, perfectly conjured up the atmosphere of early Seventies rare groove. With its soaring horn solos, electric piano and a shuffling beat, 'That Spiritual Feeling' indulged in fusion – Acid Jazz – in much the same way as *Café Bleu* had dabbled in Sixties jazz. Its original, less fluid incarnation from the aborted *Modernism: A New Decade* album was eventually heard on the Style Council box set in 1998.

FLY ON THE WALL

This beautiful, emotion-drenched acoustic ballad from the 'Uh Huh Oh Yeh' single remains one of Weller's most impressive songs. "And under my feet, There's nothing to stop my own free fall/Down and down I go/And compared to it all/I'm a fly on the wall": these were typical of Weller's lyrics of the time, the product of a sudden realisation not only of fame's precarious nature but also of his insignificance in the grand scheme of things from someone once criticised for his arrogance.

ARRIVAL TIME

Another 'Uh Huh Oh Yeh' B-side was this fidgety, sax-led Acid Jazz instrumental laced with studio trickery, sections of which also provided the odd interlude on the album.

ALWAYS THERE TO FOOL YOU

The final track on the 'Uh Huh Oh Yeh' single was 'Always There To Fool You', but this was merely an instrumental version of the title track.

EVERYTHING HAS A PRICE TO PAY

'Above The Clouds' was backed by a compelling acoustic folk-blues number, 'Everything Has A Price To Pay', which was later re-recorded in a more rootsy fashion for the film *Face* (the song was heard during the opening credits) and issued on Weller's late 1997 single, 'Mermaids'.

FEELING ALRIGHT

A faithful run through Traffic's 'Feeling Alright' revealed one of the principal influences on Weller in the early Nineties. Featuring extra vocals from Young Disciples singer Carleen Anderson and Dee C. Lee, this Dave Mason composition had been performed during the summer tour.

WILD WOOD

DATE: SEPTEMBER 1993

CHART POSITION: NO. 2

ORIGINAL LP/CD: GO! DISCS 828 435-1/2

CURRENT CD: ISLAND 828 513-2

If *Paul Weller* put the musician firmly back on course, then *Wild Wood* re-established him as one of Britain's foremost musicians. The album won Paul a wider audience, tapping into a growing fascination with British music which would come to be labelled Britpop the following year with the success of Oasis and Blur. Old Jam devotees mingled with younger fans at progressively larger venues; and record sales soared.

Without the security of Solid Bond to fall back on (the studios had been sold), Weller chose The Manor to record his second solo album, in a quaint country village named Shipton-On-Cherwell, near Oxford. The studio's residential self-containment gave Weller the freedom to settle in and, costs permitting, record when he liked. Paul also warmed to the rural ambience of the Oxfordshire countryside, the perfect setting for the type of songs he was now writing, and shacked up there throughout April and May 1993 with an entourage of musicians and producers.

Paul openly acknowledged that he was finally achieving the sound he'd been striving for since those uncertain dates back in 1990. His confidence growing, he had swapped the sharp, urban edges of The Jam and the cosmopolitan feel of The Style Council for a warm, well-rounded, some might say pastoral sound (with more than a shade of Stevie Winwood's Traffic), and lyrics were awash with elemental words like "mountains", "country", "season", "lightning", "weaver", "sunflower" and "wood". This might have suggested that Paul had shifted his political sympathies towards the environmentalists, or that he had softened with age, but neither suggestion was strictly true. In his quest to discover a new musical course, Weller had arrived at a style which he felt was authentic, which was deeply rooted in tradition and which shunned the clinical nature of modern-day digital production. The accent of the music had shifted, and the funky (acid) jazz tinges of his début were virtually absent.

It must have been some party down at the Manor – the list of guest appearances ran into double figures, as if passing friends had helped out where they could, a set-up not dissimilar to The Style Council's. "We had a great time and thank you all for it", was the message on the sleeve – and it showed. Weller played a range of instruments – guitar, bass, piano, organ, harmonica, Mellotron, Moog – supported by a core of bassist Marco Nelson and drummer Steve White. The trio were joined not only by regulars Helen Turner (organ), Jacko Peake (horns and flute) and Max Beesley (Wurlitzer), but also Mick Talbot

(organ), Dee C. Lee (backing vocals), Robert Howard (guitar) and Ocean Colour Scene's Steve Craddock (guitar) and Simon Fowler (vocals). To borrow from that old Sly Stone song, *Wild Wood* felt like a family affair – borne out by the photo of Paul, Steve and Marco with their children, sitting in the grounds of the Manor. This tradition of using a pool of musicians was, like *Wild Wood* itself, rooted in the late-Sixties/early Seventies, when artists often collaborated on each other's records.

Wild Wood was also Weller's first LP to be favourably received by the music press since *Our Favourite Shop* – the odd comment about him being 'The New Clapton' aside. Within two weeks, *Wild Wood* had sold over 100,000 copies (which was already more than *Paul Weller* had achieved) and had all but topped the charts. The album was nominated for the BPI's Brit Awards (as was Weller himself as 'Best Male Artist') and later made the short-list for the then recently-inaugurated Mercury Music Prize. *Wild Wood* was then given a second lease of life in March 1994 (in fact, it returned to the Top 5), when re-promoted with the addition of Paul's post-album single, 'Hung Up'.

SUNFLOWER

After some prevarication about choosing a new single, Weller eventually opted for 'Sunflower', issued in July 1993. He was rewarded with another Top 20 hit – but it represented more than that. This track is still regarded as his best single by many fans.

'Sunflower' began with an effects-laden guitar intro that led to compar-isons with The Beatles' 'Lucy In The Sky With Diamonds' and The Faces' 'Flying'. And Paul's powerful vocal was built upon an equally punchy guitar riff. Despite some deft touches – Jacko Peake's flute and Paul's Mellotron and Moog blips – the effect was rockier than the feel of his début LP, although the song felt like a logical progression from 'Into Tomorrow' and 'Uh Huh Oh Yeh'. Brendan Lynch metamorphised the track on 1994's 'Out Of The Sinking'

single into another of his spacey, psychedelic dance creations, 'Lynch Mob Dub'.

CAN YOU HEAL US (HOLY MAN)/HOLY MAN (REPRISE)

The vibrant, piano-driven 'Can You Heal Us (Holy Man)' loosely tackled such weighty topics as religion and death. Its mellow funk ending slowed down the riff from Edwin Starr's 'War' into a spiritu-ally-uplifting groove, which was then reprised towards the close of the LP. "I've got little time for organised religion," said Paul of the song's theme. "But I think faith is very important. I don't have absolute faith yet but I like the idea that some time I will. I come from a family of atheists, which is good in one way because it's left me clear space to make my own mind up – but I've also inherited their scepticism."

WILD WOOD

'Wild Wood' (chosen as his follow-up to 'Sunflower') was an acoustic ballad which attracted adjectives like "pastoral" and "rustic" from the music press. This was reinforced not only by its title and the song's gentle melody but also its lyrics. The line, "Find your way out/Of the wild, wild wood", seemed to advocate an escape from the stress and "traffic's boom" of urban life. The song epitomised Weller's new-found affection for the acoustic approach – just him and his guitar, and an endearingly subtle tune. Whereas the mellower songs on *Paul Weller* echoed early Seventies soul, this was rooted firmly in the singer/songwriter mould. Traces of the late Nick Drake and Neil Young could be heard, but the biggest influence seemed to be the late Tim Hardin, who Weller discovered via Small Faces' covers of his most famous songs, 'If I Were A Carpenter' and 'Red Balloon'.

INSTRUMENTAL (PTS 1 & 2)

These funky non-vocal interludes were taken from a non-album jam, 'Another New Day' (*see below*).

ALL THE PICTURES ON THE WALL

Rumours that Paul's marriage to Dee C. Lee was faltering were fuelled by the lyrics of this beautiful lament to lost love, one of *Wild Wood*'s most poignant moments: "The wasted days we could have lived/Now we're left with nothing to give". The feeling of the track harked back to *Paul Weller*; but its inclusion here offset some of the album's more histrionic moments.

HAS MY FIRE REALLY GONE OUT?

The seemingly self-questioning theme of 'Has My Fire Really Gone Out?' contrasted its good-time R&B flavour, complete with harmonica – and, as if to wipe away any insecurities, the song ended with a piercing psychedelic rock jam. If the lyrics suggested self-doubt, though, Weller's aim had actually been to stick two fingers up to his critics.

COUNTRY

'Country' was a gentle, contemplative song accompanied by acoustic guitar and a stylophone passage from Brendan Lynch which echoed David Bowie's 'Space Oddity'. "I feel the time we've yet to reach," sang Weller, "Is not yet within our belief", reiterating his sense of striving forward to some unfathomable goal in life.

HUNG UP

Recorded in just three days, this slow, plaintive song crystallised Weller's new-found popularity with his first Top 10 hit for seven years. Spoilt only by a slightly murky production, 'Hung Up' attracted comparisons with The Beatles' 'Let It Be' and featured backing vocals from Ocean Colour Scene's Simon Fowler. The naked emotion of Weller's wonderfully expressive vocal perfectly suited the forlorn, angst-ridden lyrics: "Hidden in the back seat of my head/Some place I can't remember where/I found it just by coincidence/And now I'm all hung up again."

5TH SEASON

The blustering blues rock of '5th Season', which featured Paul's long-time guitar roadie Dave Liddle, began with Weller bellowing angrily, "A storm is raging, inside my head/Why am I so lost and confused/Can't find the reason, for feeling blue". After years of decrying the idea of 'rock music', Weller found that he too *could* rock!

THE WEAVER

After speculation about its possible release at the start of the year, 'The Weaver' was finally issued in late October as the third single to be lifted from *Wild Wood*. Already a live favourite, this rousing update of British R&B was based around a pounding two-chord riff. The lyric harked back to several moments in Weller's record collection – Humble Pie's "But to follow the weaver

of dreams" lyric on their *As Safe As Yesterday Is* album and the 'Dreamweaver' of John Lennon's 'God' (on *Plastic Ono Band*), although Paul later cited an old Spooky Tooth song as the initial inspiration.

FOOT OF THE MOUNTAIN

The feel of general restlessness within the lyrics of both *Paul Weller* and *Wild Wood* was also at the root of 'Foot Of The Mountain' – "Such a long way to climb/How will I ever get up there/Though I know I must try". This captivating acoustic song formed a cornerstone of *Wild Wood*, alongside the lengthy 'Shadow Of The Sun'.

SHADOW OF THE SUN

Speaking of which, this lengthy workout was an accomplished exercise in melody and musicianship in which the band indulged in some West Coast-styled instrumental interplay, climaxing in a soaring guitar solo. It's the closest Weller has ever come to the magical jams of The Grateful Dead in their prime. The lyrics were ambiguous while retaining a common theme of Weller's 'solo' lyrics, of time passing, personal reflections on earlier feelings or conversations and an awareness of age.

MOON ON YOUR PYJAMAS

'Moon On Your Pyjamas' shared a low-key feel with a relaxed, pretty tune, and a slushy yet endearing poetic lyric written about Paul's love for his children. Fatherhood, not unusually, seems to have had a profound effect on Weller's temperament: "Through your new eyes I've come to see/How beautiful my life can be".

NON-ALBUM SONGS

ENDS OF THE EARTH

The simplicity of 'Wild Wood' was matched on its B-side by this sublime, piano-led love song, which completed the picture of a musician who somehow seemed more relaxed in himself.

THIS IS NO TIME

Another telling influence was heard on *The Weaver* EP: the shadow of Bill Withers pervaded the mellow soul/folk mix that was 'This Is No Time', co-written by Weller with Marco Nelson.

ANOTHER NEW DAY

The Weaver EP also featured the meandering, laid-back jazz shuffle of 'Another New Day', snatches from which had provided two instrumental interludes on *Wild Wood*.

THE LOVED

The single finished with this yearning acoustic ballad, 'The Loved' (originally titled 'Love Of The Loved', after an early Paul McCartney song), laced with some beautiful flute, which Paul had earlier donated to a flexidisc distributed with the weekly newspaper for the homeless, *The Big Issue*.

STANLEY ROAD

DATE: MAY 1995
CHART POSITION: NO. 1
ORIGINAL LP/CD: GO! DISCS 828 619-1/2
CURRENT CD: ISLAND 828 619-2

Paul Weller's popularity exploded in the wake of *Wild Wood*. Leading acts like Oasis and Blur cited him as a major influence and his relentless touring was paying off dividends, culminating in the release of the *Live Wood* album and three sell-out nights at London's Royal Albert Hall in autumn 1994. Recent concerts had aired several new songs – 'Whirlpool's End', 'The Changingman', 'You Do Something To Me', 'Time Passes'. But Live Wood was swiftly followed by the release of yet another fresh composition, 'Out Of The Sinking'. The song felt heavier than most of *Wild Wood*, hinting at the feel of Weller's future work.

By that time, sessions had already begun for Paul's next album, which yielded the first batch of songs in just two weeks: 'Stanley Road', 'Out Of The Sinking', 'Time Passes', The Beatles' 'Sexy Sadie', 'Whirlpool's End' and 'You Do Something To Me'. Weller then returned to the Manor around New Year 1995 to record the rest of the LP before the studio was closed for good early that summer. The sessions went well, as Steve White recalled: "That was put together with much more roadwork under our belt. We'd played a lot of the tunes on the tour and gotten them to a higher standard of confidence. So the whole recording time was very short."

For the first quarter of 1995, the Weller camp was silent – aside from a mysterious white label 12" distributed to DJs, stamped 'Lynch Mob Beats'. But that promo offered a clue as to what followed: scratched in the middle of the vinyl was a message, 'The Changingman'…

By mid-April, 'The Changingman' had been announced as the lead track of

Weller's next EP, and he performed the song on the Channel 4 music show, *The White Room*. On the same programme, Weller duetted with Noel Gallagher – Paul played piano while the Oasis guitarist nervously strummed along, singing 'Talk Tonight'. For Gallagher, the partnership was the latest of his dreams to come true. This mutual admiration society worked both ways, though: Weller was seen to be friendly with a group which would be the most popular in Britain before the year was out. And the links between the artists were strengthened when Oasis replaced their drummer with Steve White's younger brother, Alan.

The latest in a line of classic, what you might call 'groovy rock' singles (following 'Into Tomorrow', 'Uh Huh Oh Yeh', 'Sunflower' and 'The Weaver'), 'The Changingman' was a promising Top 10 hit. But its success was nothing compared with that of his new album. Named after the location of his childhood home in Woking, *Stanley Road* entered the charts at No. 1 in May and

stayed in the Top 30, by and large, for over a year. Compilations aside, it was his first LP to be awarded platinum status (for reaching 300,000 sales), and by mid-1996, *Stanley Road* had sold over a million copies and been nominated for the fourth annual Mercury Music Prize – a remarkable achievement for an album which took barely two months to record.

The album featured a familiar array of musicians, Paul again playing most of the keyboards and guitars while drawing on others where necessary. Dr. Robert, Marco Nelson and Yolanda Charles alternated on bass, and Mick Talbot and Helen Turner had popped in to play keyboards on a few songs. Now a mainstay of Paul's touring band, OCS's Steve Craddock played and sang on several tracks and producer Brendan Lynch and guitar technician Dave Liddle both lent the odd touch here and there – behind it all was Steve White on drums.

Many of the songs had a rougher edge than those on Paul's first two LPs; their grace and lightness of touch was swapped for a live, very real sound which matched the sweating, earnest, gyrating, intense figure of his live shows. Oasis's Noel Gallagher had already guested during Paul's live shows; now he added rhythm guitar on a cover of Dr. John's 'Walk On Gilded Splinters'. And he wasn't the only VIP guest. When asked by *NME* in 1993 with whom he would most like to work, Paul's answer was unequivocal: Stevie Winwood. Two years later, the ex-Traffic star played keyboards on 'Woodcutter's Son' and piano on 'Pink On White Walls'. After dismissing the idea of posing in an *Abbey Road*-style photo on a zebra crossing for the sleeve, Weller retained The Beatles theme – itself, a nod towards his early teens – by commissioning the work of one of Britain's leading artists, Peter Blake, designer of rock's most famous record cover, *Sgt. Pepper*. Blake created a colourful mosaic of images relevant to Paul's past and present, which harked back both to the sleeve of *Sgt. Pepper*, and the *objets d'art* assembled on the cover of

Our Favourite Shop.

Interspersed among the pop-art symbols were allusions to Weller's music heroes (John Lennon, Aretha Franklin, The Small Faces, Stax), fashion (a Mod astride a scooter), other interests (London, poetry, momentos of trips abroad) and, most important of all, his childhood (old holiday snaps with his parents, George Best, a local Green Line bus and, in the centre, a sign for Stanley Road behind a painting of Paul as a small boy holding a photograph of him in 1995).

The theme implied that Weller's life had come full circle. The one emotional bond which has sustained him through thick and thin has been with his parents, who took pride of place in the credits on *Stanley Road*. "I dedicate this record to my Mum and Dad, who've always been there for me and always encouraged me to follow this path," he wrote. "It's also for my wife Dee and our beautiful children." Suddenly, the idea of the boy next door didn't seem so strange.

Despite the LP's runaway success, it

elicited a cautious response from both Weller's fans and the music critics. Some of Paul's most loyal admirers were unconvinced by the album's chugging, lumpen production, which occasionally muddied the songs. Whereas a certain zing emanated from *Paul Weller* and *Wild Wood* benefited from a lightness of touch, *Stanley Road* – it was said – suffered in places from a stodgy sound and Paul's thunderous vocal technique. The album duly fared poorly in the journalists' end-of-year summaries.

THE CHANGINGMAN

There was no mistaking the autobiographical element of 'The Changingman'. The lyrics reiterated Weller's continued attempt to reach some mystical, elusive goal: "What I can't be today, I can be tomorrow". But this restlessness was also matched by the sense of confusion (what Weller called the large expanse of grey in between the black and white world of his youth) of lines like: "And the more I see, the more I know/The more I know, the less I understand". This familiar philosophical quandry was expounded in books like *Zen And The Art Of Motorcycle Maintenance* (which Paul had read years before). Applied to music, this restlessness led to his desire to write songs which, in his opinion, might achieve the same greatness as the Sixties rock classics he tried to emulate – music, to his mind, with some palpable meaning. 'The Changingman' came close, although it borrowed its subtle, descending guitar intro from ELO's '10538 Overture' – or that song's inspiration, The Beatles' 'Dear Prudence'.

Paul claimed the single's title was inspired by hearing his daughter Leah talking about one of her dolls – although it was an uncanny coincidence that a friend of Weller's managed a band of the same name. Regardless of its inspiration, though, 'The Changingman' was powerful rock record and its faint psychedelic edge managed to invoke the spirit of the late-Sixties within a modern context.

PORCELAIN GODS

'Porcelain Gods' meandered along in a manner verging on progressive rock, as its brittle melody matched the vulnerability of Paul's lyrics, questioning the nature of fame. "And how disappointed I am/To find me part of no plan," he sang with a sense of anguish, "Just a porcelain God, that shatters when it falls." Weller had fallen once but, as the song continued, "I shake it off and start again". And lines like, "Most who see me, see me not for real", and "I hate too what you hate in me", dealt with the complexities of idolatry – from the idol's point of view. A radio session version (from the Dutch station KRO Radio 3 from October 1995) was later issued on the *Out Of The Sinking* EP in early 1996.

I WALK ON GILDED SPLINTERS

'Porcelain Gods' merged into a raucous, dynamic performance of Dr. John's 'I Walk On Gilded Splinters' – though Paul probably heard the song courtesy either of Marsha Hunt, Steve Marriott (in Humble Pie) or Johnny Jenkins. Noel Gallagher's acoustic guitar contribution was lost in this claustrophobic brew of funky drums, overdriven guitars and Paul's straining-at-the-leash vocals. These songs dominated side one, creating an overriding impression that Weller was, dare it be said, rocking out.

YOU DO SOMETHING TO ME

Chosen as album's second single, this yearning lullaby sounded a tad earnest and plodding, spoiling what was otherwise an attractive melody. 'You Do Something To Me' had first been aired on the radio back in 1993, demo'd at the Manor on New Year's Day 1994 with a view to being a possible single, and recorded prior to 'Out Of The Sinking'. Promoted by a video of Weller and friends shot in the countryside around Woking, it proved to be another sizeable hit.

WOODCUTTER'S SON

The wonderful 'Woodcutter's Son' was a gruff rhythm and blues effort – a mid-Nineties take on Bo Diddley via *Exile On Main Street*-era Rolling Stones. When Weller sang, "I'm cutting down the wood for the good of everyone!", it sounded like a response to criticism that he had milked the *Wild Wood* album.

TIME PASSES...

Despite the aggressive tone of *Stanley Road*'s first three tracks, the album's ratio between loud, extrovert material and quieter, introspective ballads was roughly the same as previous efforts. One of the oldest songs on the album, the beautiful 'Time Passes...', was a mournful tale of lost love perfectly communicated by the heartfelt emotion of Weller's voice.

STANLEY ROAD

The title track was the album's central song, both physically and conceptually.

'Stanley Road' strutted along, led by Weller's strident piano riff (presumably borrowed from Van Morrison's 'Moondance'). The lyrics fitted more comfortably into the album as a whole – a nostalgic vision of the street in which Paul spent his childhood. "A hazy mist hung down the street/The length of its mile/As far as my eye could see/The sky so wide, the houses tall/Or so they seemed to be/So they seemed to me so small": Stanley Road was quite short but it would have seemed long enough for someone still in short trousers, hearing the "rolling stock" on the nearby railway.

BROKEN STONES

Less grandiose than 'You Do Something To Me' was his next single, the sublime 'Broken Stones', a softly-spoken tune which combined an endearing Al Green flavour with a neat lyrical metaphor – people are like "pebbles on a beach, kicked around, all trying to get home". A radio session version (from the Dutch station KRO

Radio 3 from October 1, 1995) was later issued on the *Out Of The Sinking* EP.

OUT OF THE SINKING

Aired as 'The Sinking' earlier in the year, this chunky rock song was firmly rooted in the early Seventies, but interrupted by a power chord crescendo which echoed prime time Steve Marriott on the Small Faces' 'Afterglow (Of Your Love)'. "I wanted to write a great English mod love song," Paul explained. "How did I feel when I wrote this? Frightened, insecure, crazy but powerful. The middle section is pure Small Faces and proud."

His current standing as one of Britain's leading performers was recognised both by the Brits (he retained the award for 'Best Male Solo Artist') and *NME*'s corresponding Brat Award. Go! Discs responded to Weller's trophies with their own tribute – a limited reissue of 'Out Of The Sinking' – the album version featuring vocal overdubs from Carleen Anderson, as opposed to the earlier single.

PINK ON WHITE WALLS

Along similar soulful lines to 'Broken Stones' was 'Pink On White Walls', a jolly, swinging R&B affair with music to match its philosophical lyrics.

WHIRLPOOLS' END

The driving intensity and psychedelic vibe of the lengthy 'Whirlpools' End' hardened up the feel of 'Shadow Of The Sun', as a worthy successor to the spaced out atmosphere of 'Kosmos'.

WINGS OF SPEED

The final song was linked to a painting on the cover. "On 'Wings Of Speed', I tried to describe the feelings I get from *The Lady Of Shallot* by John Waterhouse," Weller revealed. "I'm not an art buff – I like what I like, etc. – but the lady in the painting looks real." The tune was a graceful attempt at a gospel ballad, although the combination of piano and Carleen Anderson's choral falsetto sounded faintly grandiose.

NON-ALBUM SONGS

SEXY SADIE

First time around, 'Out Of The Sinking' was backed by a faithful run through The Beatles' 'Sexy Sadie', featuring Ocean Colour Scene bassist Damon Minchella. While this was reflected by various Beatles references on the single's back cover, the cover photo shoot and promo video (with Paul in a fur coat posing outdoors next to guitar amps) borrowed an idea from an old Small Faces clip.

I'D RATHER GO BLIND

A barroom bluesy cover of Etta James' R&B classic appeared on *The Changingman* EP, though Weller's rendition seemed to owe more to Rod Stewart's early Seventies version.

IT'S A NEW DAY, BABY

Speaking of which, traces of The Faces' rustic, good-time atmosphere could also be heard on Paul's acoustic folk-blues tune, 'It's A New Day, Baby' (again on *The Changingman* EP), one of the new songs to escape the album.

MY WHOLE WORLD IS FALLING DOWN

'You Do Something To Me' was joined on an EP by a cover of William Bell's old Stax soul classic, culled from Weller's visit to Radio One's *The Evening Session* that May.

A YEAR LATE

Paul had written three songs over that Christmas break in 1994 while staying in Woking – 'Hung Up', 'Time Passes...' and this fragile ballad, which appeared on the back of 'You Do Something To Me'.

STEAM
(alias LYNCH MOB BEATS)

Circulated in early 1995 prior to the album's release, 'Lynch Mob Beats' was another of Brendan Lynch's off-the-wall experiments in mixing funk and psychedelia, looping drum beats and a guitar riff from the bare bones of one of Paul's songs. 'Lynch Mob Beats' was

based loosely on one of the forthcoming LP tracks, 'Whirlpools' End'. Extracts appeared on Weller's next LP (at the end of side one) and the track was eventually chosen as a B-side to 'Broken Stones', now entitled 'Steam'.

I SHALL BE RELEASED

Second time around, 'Out Of The Sinking' was accompanied by a respectful cover of Bob Dylan's late-Sixties classic, 'I Shall Be Released' (as popularised by The Band), taken from the forthcoming British film, *Hollow Reed*.

HEAVY SOUL

HEAVY SOUL

DATE: JULY 1997

CHART POSITION: NO. 2

ORIGINAL CD: ISLAND CID 8058, NO. 2

Nearly two years on from the million-selling success of *Stanley Road*, there was still no sign of a follow-up. The only evidence of new material had been Paul's only release of 1996, the strutting, straightforward rock of 'Peacock Suit'. Previewed at Weller's mammoth Finsbury Park event, 'British Summer Time', and during a special *Top Of The Pops* performance, the single was finally issued that August. The rest of '96 seemed to be taken up with the *Help* project (see elsewhere), prompting the creation of supergroup the Smokin' Mojo Filters (Weller, Noel Gallagher, Paul McCartney and others) to record The Beatles' 'Come Together'. Behind the scenes, Go! Discs had been taken over by PolyGram. Unhappy about the situation, Weller eventually moved across to the Island label (the original home, after all, to influences like Nick Drake, Spooky Tooth and Traffic), before the eventual launch of Weller's new album, *Heavy Soul*, in July '97.

Each Paul Weller solo album had been progressively less smooth, less subtle. *Paul Weller* retained some of The Style Council's polish; *Wild Wood* dropped the acid jazz tinges for an earthier feel; and *Stanley Road* was characterised by its solid 'live' production. And to paraphrase a TV advert, *Heavy Soul* did exactly what it said on the cover.

Recorded early in '97 at Van Morrison's Woolhall Studios in Bath, *Heavy Soul* appeared to be a logical development of Weller's obsession with a back-to-basics approach – but maybe he'd gone too far. Its jagged edges were off-putting, rather as if we'd been given a rough-and-ready prototype instead of the finished album. Perversely enough, Paul had already introduced a new backing band – Matt Deighton (ex-frontman with

Acid Jazz act Mother Earth) on rhythm guitar and Yolanda Charles back on bass – who should have lent a funkier edge to the sound than that of the Ocean Colour Scene guitarists.

Initially, the lyrics within *Heavy Soul* felt difficult to decipher and instruments sounded buried beneath the album's claustrophobic production. In attempting to convey the bruised emotion of British blueswailers like, say, Steve Marriott or Joe Cocker, Paul's voice seemed wayward and off-key. The songs tended to be built upon a solid platform of guitar riffs rather than overtly tuneful melodies and the rhythm section all too often felt lacklustre. And the whole effect felt too earnest, too serious, too... well, heavy. But if its heavier soul workouts dominate the ears, then the album's most accomplished tunes were those of a less upfront nature. In fact, *Heavy Soul* was a more carefully crafted affair than first impressions suggested.

The whole package was strongly rooted in a Sixties/Seventies rock crossover – from the artwork depicting the album title in post-*Rubber Soul* psychedelic writing to the late Sixties pink Island label design. Gone were the rose-tinted reminiscences of his Woking childhood that adorned *Wild Wood* and *Stanley Road*: "Like all nostalgia, it wears thin after a while," he admitted in 1996. "I've stayed in Woking quite a lot this year-and-a-half. It was nice at first but I've got a bit bored now – the nostalgic part has run its course. But I suppose there always comes a point when people go back and plug in again to their roots. It's been twenty years since I left Woking – at that time, I couldn't wait to get away!"

Bearing in mind Paul's other working title for the album, *Raving R&B*, it seemed clear in which direction Weller is heading. Coupled with traces of Free, Humble Pie, Sixties Stax soul and The Faces within the music, this invariably led some critics to pan the musician for adopting what they deemed to be a retrogressive stance: 'Dad Rock', as it had already been tagged. But Weller's records have rarely had an outward immediacy and *Heavy Soul* had a depth which only became evident after repeated exposure.

HEAVY SOUL/ HEAVY SOUL PT. 2

The two-part title track, 'Heavy Soul', sounded like an anguished battle cry, all angst-ridden R&B and claustrophobic guitar riffs. Its bullish blues picked up where 'Porcelain Gods' left off, while the lyrics could easily be applied to his conflict with PolyGram: "I'm touched by the thought that I can't be bought/ 'Cause I'm a heavy soul".

PEACOCK SUIT

The production of this pre-emptive strike from *Heavy Soul* was tougher and more aggressive than most of *Stanley Road*, as Weller growled and barked in a throwback to the 'angry' days of The Jam. An intense, masculine R&B work-out, 'Peacock Suit' was played hard and fast; only the groovy funk-rock refrain at the end softened the blow. The song's stripped-bare approach was perfectly captured by the promotional video, Weller and Craddock duelling on Rickenbackers (including Paul's distinctive pop-art guitar, another nod to his past) in a spartan, brick-walled basement. Indeed, Weller viewed the song as his ultimate mod expression.

UP IN SUZE'S ROOM

'Up In Suze's Room' was a mesmerising, atmospheric song (though the listener was none the wiser as to the identity of the lady in question), unveiled during shows and TV appearances in late '96. It was also performed during a surprise acoustic support slot from Paul at one of soul singer (and fellow Go! Discs artist) Gabrielle's shows at Soho's legendary jazz club Ronnie Scott's, alongside 'Waiting On An Angel' (by U.S. singer/songwriter Ben Harper) and Ocean Colour Scene's 'The Circle'. 'Suze's Room' even seemed to echo the jazz/R&B crossover of *Café Bleu*-era Style Council.

BRUSHED

'Brushed' was an intense rollercoaster of blues funk, Weller's aggressive hollering offset by some searing guitar stabs and electronic mischief from oscillator operator Brendan Lynch.

DRIVING NOWHERE

The acoustic 'Driving Nowhere' had a mournful quality and that introspective Sunday feeling which matched lyrics like, "I'm still drifting, I've got no faith". This and 'Up In Suze's Room' were two of the earliest songs to be completed: demos were circulating within Go! Discs prior to the release of 'Peacock Suit'.

I SHOULD HAVE BEEN THERE TO INSPIRE YOU

This lengthy piano ballad had a country-ish flavour, a mature, smoky barroom lament in the vein of 'Wings Of Speed'. Weller has made no secret of its subject matter: his now ex-wife Dee C. Lee.

FRIDAY STREET

More buoyantly melodic was 'Friday Street' (as in 'Friday On My Mind' and 'Dead End Street'), a pleasantly flowing song and a less literal extension of the 'Stanley Road' idea. One of the most accessible songs on the album made for a fitting single release, promoted by a video in which Weller revisited his old Woking home in Balmoral Drive on the Maybury Estate, parka-clad and riding on an old Lambretta.

SCIENCE

'Science' boasted a crisp, snappy drumbeat, the perfect backdrop for the song's light, floating atmosphere as Paul returned to his lyrical quest for a sense of identity: "I can be who I am/I have no pretence".

GOLDEN SANDS

Ploughing a parallel Stonesy vein, 'Golden Sands' was Paul's brashest take on late-Sixties Stax R&B, evoking the hazy Southern States heat with a stomping soul rhythm and some gliding, Dr. John-like electric piano.

AS YOU LEAN INTO THE LIGHT

The most endearing, enduring moment on *Heavy Soul*, 'As You Lean Into The Light' was an atmospheric tune (file under 'Country'), dreamy and softly spoken one moment, hoarse and defiant at others. An alternate acoustic version was made available on the *Brushed* EP.

MERMAIDS

The Van Morrison-like 'Mermaids' shared this refreshingly tuneful edge, with its loose rhythm, jangly guitar and an anthemic "sha la-la la-la" chorus (which flirted dangerously with the feel of some pub rock singalong). Dedicated to "anyone from the Home Counties", 'Mermaids' harked back to The Style Council in their heyday (albeit performed in a more gutsy manner) and, again, made perfect sense as a single.

NON-ALBUM SONGS

EYE OF THE STORM

More Brendan Lynch studio trickery was behind this warped instrumental, which was the only accompaniment on the 'Peacock Suit' single.

AIN'T NO LOVE IN THE HEART OF THE CITY

One of Paul's most powerful, impressive covers was this mid-Seventies Bobby Bland classic from his LP *The Dreamer*. It was tucked away on 'Brushed', one of several 7"s under the banner of *A Heavy Soul EP*.

SHOOT THE DOVE

Another of the 'Brushed' companions was 'Shoot The Dove', which began with a piano intro not a million miles from John Lennon's 'Imagine' but evolved into a melancholy tune in the vein of 'Hung Up'.

SO YOU WANT TO BE
A DANCER

This lengthy, instrumental B-side to 'Mermaids' sounded like a mod version of The Prodigy, as Brendan Lynch and engineer Martin 'Max' Heyes cut up all manner of psychedelic goings on, from computer trickery to warped guitar sounds, over a funky, insistent backbeat.

BRAND NEW START

Weller's sole new offering in 1998 was this gentle, rootsy song that secured once and for all Weller's link to the more mature British blues of Eric Clapton – or even the gruff jazz-blues of John Martyn – with shades of Lennon's 'Jealous Guy' or Neil Young's 'Heart Of Gold'. 'Brand New Start' was the exclusive non-album carrot dangled to buyers of the inevitable hits collection, *Modern Classics*, issued that autumn.

THE RIVERBANK

Never has a contrast been so striking in Weller's career as the combination of 'Brand New Start' (in which Weller appeared to be creating some Anglo-American, folk blues-based hybrid) and 'The Riverbank', a subtle, beguiling rewrite of the old Jam classic, 'Tales From The Riverbank', which sounded just about as English as things got. Weller had occasionally returned to 'Riverbank' over the years (not least on a *Later With Jools Holland* special), but the decision to re-record the song was unusual for one who has so defiantly avoided his earlier musical incarnations. And yet, in some small way, it brings this book full circle, with lyrics inspired by Paul's memories of the Surrey country-side during his childhood.

SMOKIN' MOJO FILTERS & INDIAN VIBES
(WELLER'S MODS'N'SODS)

DON'T LET ME DOWN

An earnest, powerful treatment of the late-Sixties Beatles classic was donated to a Fab Four covers LP, *Revolution No. 9* (Pop God PGLP 09, 1991), to raise money for Oxfam's Cambodia appeal.

COME TOGETHER by the SMOKIN' MOJO FILTERS

Paul was approached to contribute to a fund-raising album for Brian Eno's War Child charity, which had been founded to help alleviate the suffering of children in war-torn Bosnia. Co-ordinated by Weller's then record label, Go! Discs, the *Help* album was recorded in just one day – September 4, 1995 – in different studios around the country by an array of Britain's leading performers, such as Blur, Oasis and Massive Attack. Although the package was anonymous (the different artists weren't credited with the individual contributions), the figurehead of the compilation was undoubtedly a supergroup collective disguised by the moniker of The Smokin' Mojo Filters.

The group's line-up was heralded as the meeting of three generations – Paul Weller, Paul McCartney (guitar, piano, backing vocals), and Noel Gallagher (guitar). Weller explained to *NME* how he roped in the ex-Beatle: "I wrote him a letter about doing the track a while ago and he's just come down and helped us out."

The band assembled to record The Beatles' 'Come Together' in the very studio where the song was originally laid down, Abbey Road's famous Studio 2. "We've been jamming it in our sound-checks for ages," Weller added. It felt like a momentous occasion to all involved, a feeling expressed by Paolo Hewitt, who shot home video footage of the event, capturing the whole recording, together with visitors to the studio like supermodel Kate Moss and actor

Johnny Depp.

Their rendition was solid enough, but the musical worth of the group's performance wasn't the issue. Five days after the session, *Help* made history as the fastest album ever to reach the shops. Sales of some 71,000 copies on its first day of release would have ensured Go! Discs' claim that *Help* was the quickest album to reach No. 1 – if chart regulations hadn't excluded 'various artists' LPs.

Early in December, 'Come Together' was issued as the lead song on an EP, alongside other contributions from The Beautiful South, Dodgy and Black Grape. Go! Discs probably left its release too late and the single was drowned in the hectic pre-Christmas market, but the sentiment was sound enough. Weller may have lost his past dedication to playing benefit concerts and political rallies, disillusioned with the way in which his wider views interfered with people's appreciation of his music – but he was still willing to contribute to such an unequivocal project.

MATHAR by INDIAN VIBES

Weller played electric sitar, plus acoustic and electric guitar on this cover of 'Mathar', by then already a club favourite written by German jazz guitarist Volker Kriegel, and originally released by the Dave Pike Set on European label MPS Records in 1969. Also featuring Marco Nelson and Galliano's Crispin Taylor and produced by Brendan Lynch, 'Mathar' was issued in September 1994 by Virgin France (most mixes are best described as dabbling in techno), before being reissued in 1998 with new remixes.

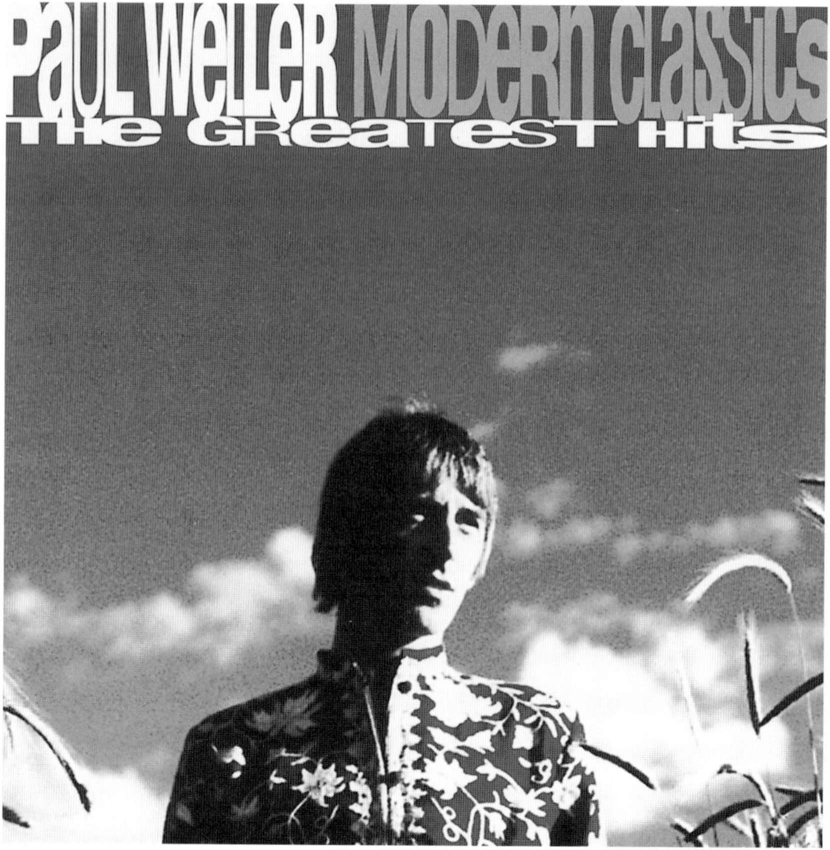
PAUL WELLER MODERN CLASSICS
THE GREATEST HITS

PAUL WELLER:
COMPILATION ALBUMS

MODERN CLASSICS:
THE GREATEST HITS

RELEASE DATE: OCTOBER 1998,

CHART POSITION: NO. 7

CURRENT CD: ISLAND CIDD 8080

If anything, this 'best of' seemed to jump the gun - after all, wasn't it just a contactual obligation affair delivered so that Weller could move over from Island to Independiente (run by his old friends from Go! Discs). Well, partly. But all sixteen tracks were Top 40 hits, if you include the one new offering, 'Brand New Start' (see elsewhere), a remarkable achievement for someone who had already notched up his fair share with two previous bands. Initial copies of *Modern Classics* came with a free CD entitled *Live Classics* (see the Paul Weller Live section for more details).

The track listing of *Modern Classics* is as follows:
'Out Of The Sinking' / 'Peacock Suit' / 'Sunflower' / 'The Weaver' / 'Wild Wood' / 'Above The Clouds' / 'Uh Huh Oh Yeh' / 'Brushed' / 'The Changingman' / 'Friday Street' / 'You Do Something To Me' / 'Brand New Start' / 'Hung Up' / 'Mermaids' / 'Broken Stones' / 'Into Tomorrow'

PAUL WELLER LIVE

LIVE WOOD

DATE: SEPTEMBER 1994

CHART POSITION: NO. 13

ORIGINAL 2-LP/CD: GO! DISCS 828 561-1/2

CURRENT CD: ISLAND 828 561-2

The track listing of *Live Wood* is as follows: 'Bull-Rush'-'Magic Bus' / 'This Is No Time' / 'All The Pictures On The Wall' / 'Remember How We Started'-'Dominoes' / 'Above The Clouds' / 'Wild Wood' / 'Shadow Of The Sun' / '(Can You Heal Us) Holy Man'-'War' / '5th Season' / 'Into Tomorrow' / 'Foot Of The Mountain' / 'Sunflower' / 'Has My Fire Really Gone Out?'

EXCLUSIVE SONGS

MAGIC BUS

Part of The Who's 1968 classic was stapled on the end of 'Bull-Rush', acting as a fitting climax to one of the highlights of Weller's debut album. An earlier version of this amalgam (taped at the Royal Albert Hall in October 1992) had already graced 1993's 'Sunflower' single.

DOMINOES

This mid-Seventies jazz-funk classic (originally recorded by jazz legend Donald Byrd) was borrowed by Weller to end 'Remember How We Started'.

NON-ALBUM SONGS

ALL YEAR ROUND

A jazzy update of The Style Council's 'All Year Round', captured on stage that summer in New York City's The Ritz in July 1992 can be found on the single 'Above The Clouds'.

OHIO

Neil Young had written 'Ohio' in 1970 in response to the shooting of demonstrators at Ohio's Kent State University, and recorded the song with America's most successful supergroup of the period, Crosby, Stills, Nash and Young. Weller's live cover reflected his interest in this era, but while his thunderous performance was solid enough, the song's attacking lyrical content only emphasised the lack of a similar drive among Paul's own material. A recording from the Royal Albert Hall from October 1992 surfaced on *The Weaver* EP.

During a later performance of the song at the same venue, Bernard Butler joined Weller onstage to guest on guitar.

FOOT OF THE MOUNTAIN

(Live at Royal Albert Hall 23/11/93) Another Albert Hall recording (this time from November 1993) appeared on the 'Hung Up' single: an extended live treatment of one of the cornerstones of *Wild Wood*.

I DIDN'T MEAN TO HURT YOU

The Royal Albert Hall was again the setting for this in-concert take of the sublime 'I Didn't Mean To Hurt You' (from *Wild Wood*), which turned up on 'The Changingman' single.

THIS IS NO TIME

A various artists cassette, *NME Brat Pack '95* (given away with 28.1.95 issue of *NME*) featured a Royal Albert Hall version of 'This Is No Time', an impressive B-side to 'The Weaver'.

SUNFLOWER
BRUSHED
MERMAIDS

To promote *Heavy Soul*, Paul and his band set up their gear on top of one of the Southbank buildings on a warm summer evening and rattled through a forty-minute set – including these three highlights on the 'Friday Street' single. A promotional-only, semi-official vinyl 'bootleg' of the show was also circulated.

OTHER LIVE
COVER VERSIONS

Weller has often dabbled in cover versions outside the studio. For example, Paul guested with Dr. Robert at Harlesden's Mean Fiddler Acoustic Room for an encore of two Tim Hardin songs, 'Red Balloon' and 'Reason To Believe', and played guitar on a rendition of T. Rex's 'Life's A Gas'. And on his first-ever solo tour, he covered the Isley Brothers' 'Work To Do'.

LIVE CLASSICS

RELEASE DATE: OCTOBER 1998

CURRENT CD: FREE WITH INITIAL COPIES OF *MODERN CLASSICS*

(2-CD, ISLAND CIDD 8080)

Weller's solo career has been characterised by an increasing love of playing live, so it was fitting that the first solo Weller 'best of' should be accompanied - initially, at least - with a live album. It didn't say so on the package but *Live Classics* was recorded at Weller's Victoria Park show from August 1997.

The track listing of *Live Classics* is as follows:

'Into Tomorrow' / 'Peacock Suit' / 'Friday Street' / 'Mermaids' / 'Out Of The' Sinking'/'Heavy Soul' / 'Wild Wood' / 'Up In Suze's Room' / '(Can You Hear Us) Holy Man?' / 'The Changingman' / 'Porcelain Gods' / 'Sunflower' / 'Broken Stones'

Index